THEMATIC UNIT
NATIVE AMERICANS
Primary

Written by Leigh Severson

Illustrated by Blanca Apodaca, Cheryl Buhler, Sue Fullam, and Keith Vasconcelles

Teacher Created Materials, Inc.
P.O. Box 1040
Huntington Beach, CA 92647
©1991 Teacher Created Materials, Inc.
Made in U.S.A.

ISBN 1-55734-276-8

Table of Contents

Introduction

Native Americans is a captivating, whole language, thematic unit. Its 80 exciting reproducible pages are filled with a wide variety of lesson ideas designed for use with primary children. At its core are three high-quality children's literature selections, *Arrow to the Sun*, *Rainbow Crow*, and *The Legend of the Bluebonnet*. For these books activities are included which set the stage for reading, encourage the enjoyment of the book, and extend the concepts gained. In addition, the theme is connected to the curriculum with activities in language arts (including daily writing suggestions), math, science, social studies, art, music, and life skills (cooking, physical education, etc.) Many of these activites encourage cooperative learning. Suggestions and patterns for bulletin boards and unit management tools are additional time savers for the busy teacher. Furthermore, directions for student-created Big Books and a culminating activity, which allow students to synthesize their knowledge in order to produce products that can be shared beyond the classroom, highlight this very complete teacher resource.

This thematic unit includes:

- ☐ **literature selections** — summaries of three children's books with related lessons (complete with reproducible pages) that cross the curriculum

- ☐ **poetry** — suggested selections and lessons enabling students to write and publish their own works

- ☐ **planning guides** — suggestions for sequencing lessons each day of the unit

- ☐ **writing ideas** — daily suggestions as well as writing activities across the curriculum, including Big Books

- ☐ **bulletin board ideas** — suggestions and plans for student-created and/or interactive bulletin boards

- ☐ **homework suggestions** — extending the unit to the child's home

- ☐ **curriculum connections** — in language arts, math, science, social studies, art, music, and life skills such as cooking and physical education

- ☐ **group projects** — to foster cooperative learning

- ☐ **a culminating activity** — which requires students to synthesize their learning to produce a product or engage in an activity that can be shared with others

- ☐ **a bibliography** — suggesting additional literature and nonfiction books on the theme

---

To keep this valuable resource intact so that it can be used year after year, you may wish to punch holes in the pages and store them in a three-ring binder.

Introduction *(cont.)*

Why Whole Language?

A whole language approach involves children in using all modes of communication: reading, writing, listening, observing, illustrating, experiencing, and doing. Communication skills are interconnected and integrated into lessons that emphasize the whole of language rather than isolating its parts. The lessons revolve around selected literature. Reading is not taught as a separate subject from writing and spelling, for example. A child reads, writes (spelling appropriately for his/her level), speaks, listens, etc. in response to a literature experience introduced by the teacher. In this way, language skills grow naturally, stimulated by involvement and interest in the topic at hand.

Why Thematic Planning?

One very useful tool for implementing an integrated whole language program is thematic planning. By choosing a theme with correlating literature selections for a unit of study, a teacher can plan activities throughout the day that lead to a cohesive, in-depth study of the topic. Students will be practicing and applying their skills in meaningful contexts. Consequently, they tend to learn and retain more. Both teachers and students will be freed from a day that is broken into unrelated segments of isolated drill and practice.

Why Cooperative Learning?

Besides academic skills and content, students need to learn social skills. No longer can this area of development be taken for granted. Students must learn to work cooperatively in groups in order to funciton well in modern society. Group activities should be a regular part of school life and teachers should consciously include social objectives as well as academic objectives in their planning. For example, a group working together to write a report may need to select a leader. The teacher should make clear to the students and monitor the qualities of good leader-follower group interaction just as he/she would state and monitor the academic goals of the project.

Why Big Books?

An excellent cooperative, whole language activity is the production of Big Books. Groups of students, or the whole class, can apply their language skills, content knowledge, and creativity to produce a Big Book that can become a part of the classroom library to be read and reread. These books make excellent culminating projects for sharing beyond the classroom with parents, librarians, other classes, etc. Big Books can be produced in many ways and this thematic unit book includes directions for at least one method you may choose.

Arrow to the Sun

by Gerald McDermott

Summary

Arrow to the Sun is an adaptation of a Pueblo Indian tale. It tells of a young boy who is actually the son of the sun. Since he has no earthly father, the other children tease him. When he is old enough, he goes in search of his father. An arrow maker shapes him into an arrow and sends him to the sun. There he has to prove his bravery by passing four tests. Finally, he returns to his village with the power of the sun. The entire population celebrates his return with the Dance of Life.

This book received the Caldecott Award for its bold and colorful illustrations. Children enjoy them, but they need a teacher's assistance to really understand and appreciate the story. It is well worth the effort!

The outline below is a suggested plan for using the various activities that are presented in this unit. You may adapt these ideas to fit your own classroom.

Sample Plan

DAY I

- Daily Writing Activities (pages 43-47)
- Individual Pueblo Village art (page 8)
- Pueblo village mural (page 6)
- Start collecting odds and ends for kachina dolls (pages 62-63)

DAY II

- Daily Writing Activities (pages 43-47)
- Prediction chart (see page 7)
- Teacher read aloud (first half of book)
- Co-op or partner created kivas (page 9)
- Poetry writing (page 37)
- Growing Corn (page 52)

DAY III

- Daily Writing Activities (pages 43-47)
- Teacher reread first half of the story (students accompany with pantomime and sound effects)
- Finish reading the story — check back with prediction chart
- Kiva Sequencing (page 10)

DAY IV

- Daily Writing Activities (pages 43-47)
- Share homework
- Prepare flannel board or stick puppet presentation (pages 7, 11, 12)
- Make spool kachina doll (pages 62-63)

DAY V

- Daily Writing Activities (pages 43-47)
- Present flannel board story or stick puppet play for another class or group of students
- Sand Painting (pages 59-60)

Overview of Activities

SETTING THE STAGE

1. Introduce Attendance Graphing/ Daily Writing Activities. Complete directions and activities are on pages 43-47.

2. Have pictures of Pueblo housing on display. Introduce and explain the term Kiva which is a ceremonial room reserved for religious occasions.

3. If you are using the wall chart suggested in the Unit Management section (page 75), add information about the Pueblo tribes. They are located in the Southwestern area; they traveled primarily by foot; their staple food was corn (this is referred to in the story); and they were cultivators.

4. If the children are keeping their own chart, have them color in the southwestern section on the map (page 76). Locate it on the map of the United States. Discuss how far that area is from where they live. Have them fill in the rest of their chart with words or pictures.

5. Make a mural of a Pueblo village. This will be used later with stick puppets to act out the story.

   To make this mural you will need:

   > one sheet of 9" x 12" tan construction paper per child; earth tone colors of chalk (yellow, brown, orange, red); one tissue per child; large sheet of dark butcher paper (about 3ft. x 6ft./1m X 2m); glue

   Directions: Rub one piece of chalk on the construction paper. Then take the tissue and blend the color into the paper so the color is subtle. Place and glue each student's piece onto the butcher paper to make a village scene. Add ladders and windows with either chalk or brown crayons.

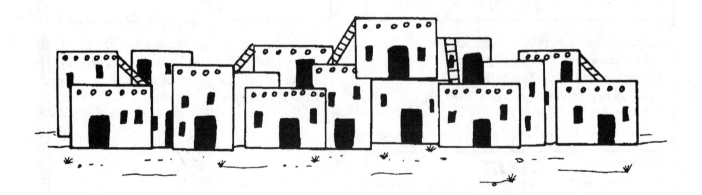

6. Have the students make their own Pueblo villages. The directions and pattern are on page 8.

7. Send home a letter requesting odds and ends for kachina dolls. You will need material scraps, feathers, old jewelry, and empty spools (optional).

6

Overview of Activities *(cont.)*

ENJOYING THE BOOK

1. Continue with Daily Writing Activities 1-3.

2. Show the cover of *Arrow to the Sun* to the students. Have them predict what the story might be about. Record their predictions on a chart and save.

3. Gather the students around you to read the first half of the story. Read until you get to the Kivas but don't tell them what is in each Kiva.

4. Give them the Kiva paper (page 9) and have them draw what they predict might be in the Kivas.

5. After drawing, have them explain their Kiva to the group. Record their Kiva predictions on the prediction chart.

6. Review the prediction chart. If the students' predictions can be grouped, graph the information.

7. Assign My Kiva (page 9) for homework. Explain that the boy in the story will have to go through something he is afraid of to prove that he is brave. Ask them to draw in their Kiva something that they were once afraid of but are not now (such as the dark, monsters under the bed, etc.). Share some of your early fears so they can feel comfortable.

8. Before continuing on in the book, review the predictions chart and have students who are willing share their own Kivas.

9. Reread the first half of the story while the students pantomime and add sound effects. This will help to review and set the scene.

10. Read to the end of the story. Have the children do the Kiva Sequencing paper (page 10) in either cooperative groups or pairs. Save the papers to be used with the stick puppets during the story retelling time.

11. Do poetry writing. Use the Color Poem from pages 38 and 39. This poem is written after coloring a pot. It relates directly back to the pot maker in the story. It is particularly appropriate because the Pueblo tribes are famous for their beautiful pottery.

12. Display the pot pictures and the color poems in a class Big Book or on a bulletin board.

EXTENDING THE BOOK

1. Make stick puppets for the book characters in cooperative groups. Patterns are on pages 11 and 12.

2. Cut out some of the Kiva sequencing pictures and put them in order on the Pueblo Village mural.

3. Have the children use their stick puppets to retell the story using the mural as a stage backdrop.

4. If you and the students want to formalize the puppet show, have them practice and then perform for another class or video tape the play for themselves.

5. Study about kachinas. Make kachina dolls (pages 62-63).

6. Study about sand painting. Make one. This could be a group or an individual project (pages 59-60).

To Make a Pueblo Village

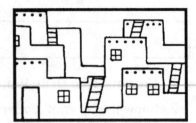

Materials:(per person) 9"x 12" white construction paper; yellow, orange, and brown chalk; facial tissue; pictures of pueblo villages for reference; pattern (below); newspaper; construction paper scraps

Directions:

1. Cut out pattern. Trace on scrap construction paper. Label top.

2. Lay newspaper over work space.

3. Color bottom ½ of construction paper pattern with yellow chalk. Go side to side. Do that several times.

4. Lay pattern across paper as shown.

5. Hold in place. With tissue gently rub from the top of the pattern to the bottom of the white paper. This will smear the yellow chalk downward.

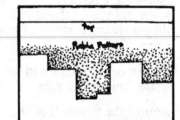

6. Repeat step 3 with orange chalk. Move pattern down and to the right about 2-2 ½" and repeat step 5. Orange should blend with yellow.

7. Do the same thing one last time with brown chalk.

8. Add details with fine line black marker.

9. Go over the top of each color with brown chalk to outline home.

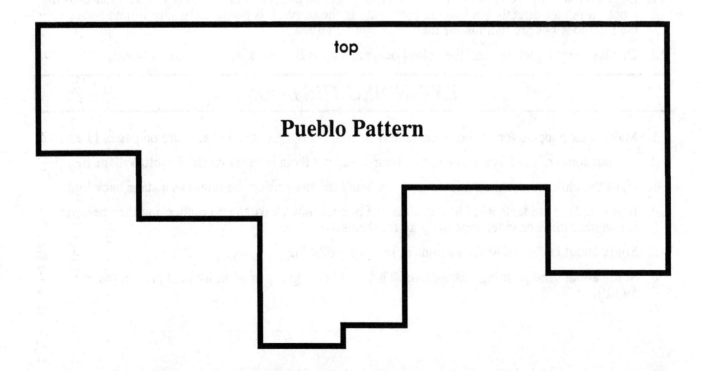

top

Pueblo Pattern

Name _____

My Kiva

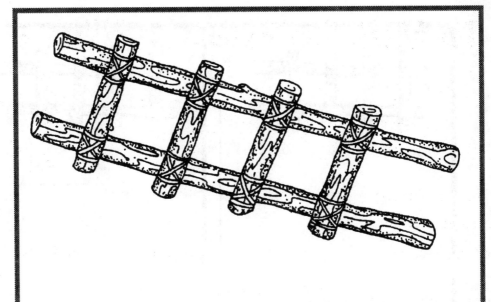

Draw what would be in your Kiva.

Note to the teacher: This will be used in two activities.

Kiva Sequencing

Name _____

The boy had to go through 4 kivas. Draw them in order.

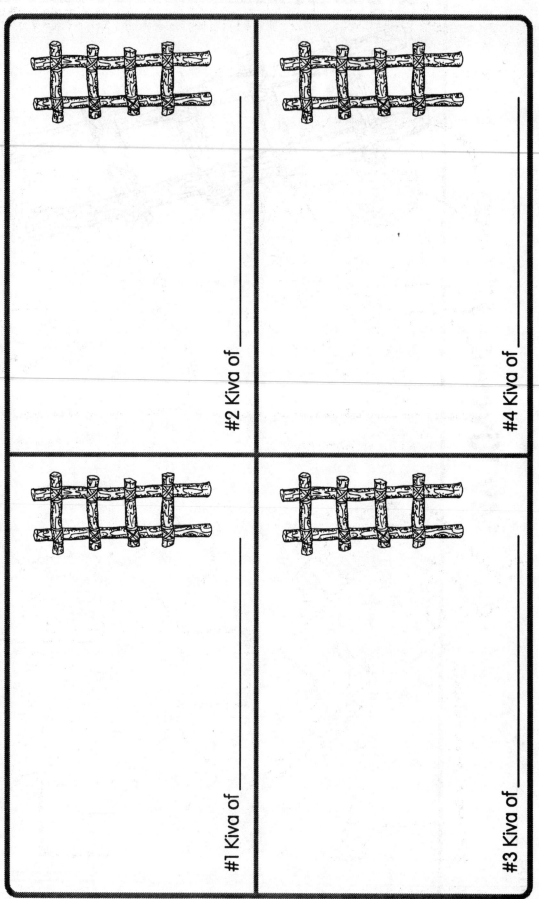

#1 Kiva of _____

#2 Kiva of _____

#3 Kiva of _____

#4 Kiva of _____

10

Arrow to the Sun Patterns

Use these patterns to make stick puppets or flannel board characters to use in retelling *Arrow to the Sun*.

Arrow Maker

Pot Maker

Corn Planter

Sun

Arrow to the Sun Patterns *(cont.)*

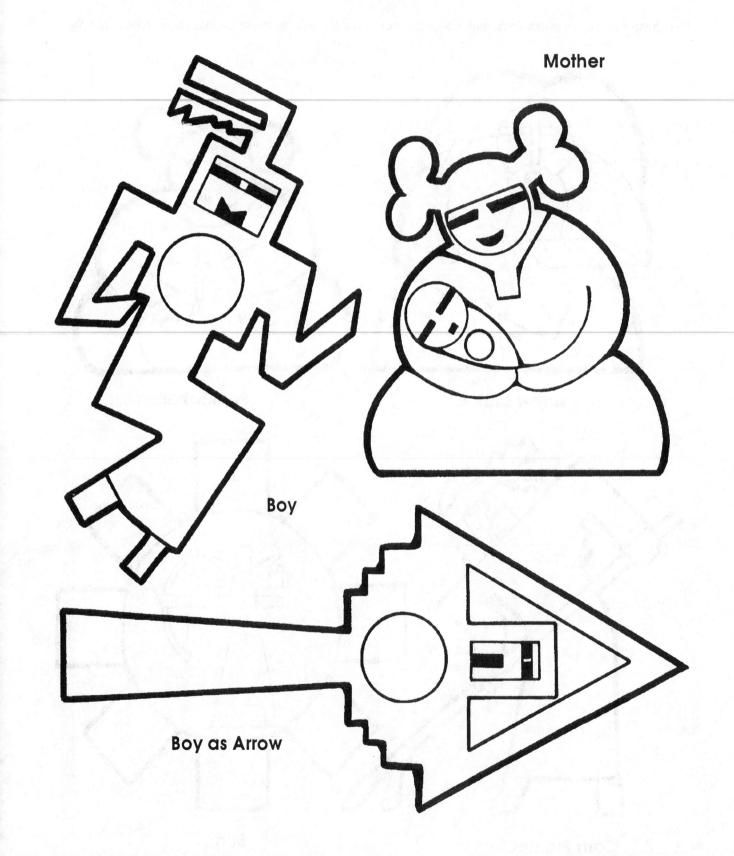

Mother

Boy

Boy as Arrow

12

Rainbow Crow

retold by Nancy Van Laan

Summary

This Native American tale comes from the Lenape tribe of the Eastern Woodlands located primarily in Eastern Pennsylvania. Many tribes have legends explaining how man first was given fire by the Great Spirit. In this tale fire was first given to the animals who were here, "Long, long ago, before the Two-Legged walked the Earth, . . ."

It was the time of the earth's first snowfall. At first the animals were not afraid but as the snow continued, it began to cover up the smaller animals. After some discussion, the animals decided to send Rainbow Crow to the Great Sky Spirit for help. Fortunately Rainbow Crow is brave and sacrificing and thus the animals of the earth are saved.

Sample Plan

Day I

- Write and illustrate favorite colors
- Make Rainbow Poem Books (page 37)
- Make a snowflake (page 14)
- Add Lenape tribe to Wall Chart and map

Day II

- Daily Writing Activities (pages 43-47)
- Read the first part of the book
- Learn about animals of the Eastern Woodlands
- Create Native American symbols (pages 16-17)
- Predict in partners: Which animal will go to the Great Sky Spirit? (page 18)

Day III

- Share predictions
- Read the end of the book
- Memorize some of the chants in the book
- Practice the chants with drum accompaniment
- Make a Rainbow Crow (pages 19-20)

Days IV and V

- Create a Rainbow Crow play (pages 21-24)
  Design and organize scenery and props
  Decide on directions and staging
  Make costumes
  Write and send invitations

Any Day During the Unit

- Learn about the Eastern Woodland tribes
- Make a canoe (pages 54-55)
- Add to the tribal map and chart (pages 75-76)

Overview of Activities

SETTING THE STAGE
---

1. Do Attendance Graphing activity #1 for *Rainbow Crow* on favorite colors. Have the students draw three things that are that color. Write or tell a friend about their choice.

2. Make Rainbow Poem Books from the poetry section (pages 37, 40, and 41). Save these and use as a bulletin board display.

3. Add the Lenape tribe to your Native American wall chart. They are an Eastern Woodlands tribe (not a major tribe); they traveled by foot and canoe; they ate mostly what they could trap or hunt; they lived in long houses not tepees. The Lenape were located in Eastern Pennsylvania.

4. Find the area on a map of the United States and compare that location with where the students live. How far is that from where they live? Have them fill in their own chart with pictures or words.

5. Explain that the climate of the area is very cold in the winter. There is a lot of snow.

6. Have the students each make at least one snowflake. Have them fold a square piece of paper into fourths. Cut pieces from each edge . To make the snowflakes sparkle, paint them with salt paint which is made by combining ⅓ cup flour, ⅓ cup salt, and water to make the mixture thick. Keep the snowflakes for the play that culminates the study of the book.

ENJOYING THE BOOK
---

1. Have the children describe or draw a crow. Let them share their thinking. They should come up with the description that a crow is a fairly large, black bird that says caw.

2. Let them know that this story will tell them how the crow that they know came to be.

3. Read the first half of the story to the class. Stop at the part where the animals discuss who should go to the Great Sky Spirit.

4. Have the students predict on a graph or chart which animal they think will go. Record and discuss the reasons for their answers.

5. Complete the Native American Picture Dictionary (pages16-17) to learn about the Eastern Woodlands animals. Help the children with the first few symbols. There is no correct answer. A Native American symbol uses an animal's basic shape or attribute. Then research to learn more about these animals.

Overview of Activities *(cont.)*

ENJOYING THE BOOK *(cont.)*

6. Extend the students' predictions by having partners do Who Should See the Great Sky Spirit? (page 18). The children can dictate or use their own invented spelling to complete the paper.

7. Before finishing the book, have the partners share their papers from # 6.

8. Read the rest of the book to the students. Have them join in the crow's caw sounds at the end.

9. Have the students practice and memorize some of the easier chants from the book. Have them say them while other students beat drums. (See Musical Instruments, pages 67-68.) Tape the chants and play them back.

10. Make a Rainbow Crow. There are three different ideas and a pattern on pages 19 and 20. Select the one that is suitable for your students.

EXTENDING THE BOOK

1. Produce a Rainbow Crow Play. This book lends itself to a quick and easy play that can be done by primary children. Divide your class in half. Half can make the mural and the other half can make the costumes. Complete directions can be found on pages 21-24.

2. Practice the play with half the students as the audience. Then switch the cast and the audience so that all students have an opportunity to act.

3. Make invitations and invite parents or other classes. Don't forget the custodian, principal, and other support personnel.

4. Video tape the play if possible. Children love to see themselves and they learn more from the experience. It's great for Open House or Parent Night.

5. Extend into science and learn about rainbows.

6. If available, share real crow feathers. You actually can see the colors as you fan through the feather.

7. Make the canoe project on pages 54-55.

8. Do the games from the physical education section that come from the Eastern Woodlands especially Danger Signal (page 69).

Native American Picture Dictionary

Animals of the Eastern Woodlands

The Native American did not have a written language with alphabet letters. He used symbols often written on rocks, on hides, or in caves. The symbols for animals often resembled the outline of the animal or a special identifying attribute.

Here are some examples:

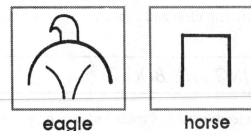  

| **eagle** | **horse** | **turtle** | **bear** |

The animals in the tale of the Rainbow Crow are all from the Eastern Woodlands area. Look at their shapes and features. Decide on a symbol for each animal and draw it next to the animal.

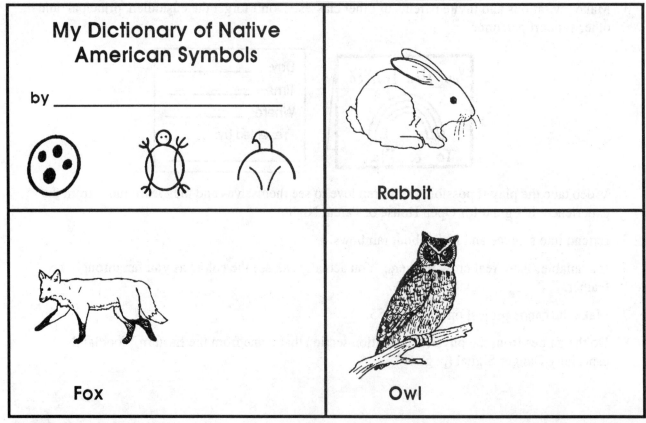

My Dictionary of Native American Symbols

by _____

Rabbit

Fox

Owl

16

Native American Picture
Dictionary *(cont.)*

Deer	**Beaver**
Squirrel	**Mouse**
Coyote	**Skunk**
Possum	**Moose**

Who Should See the Great Sky Spirit?

We think the

should go to see the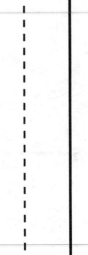

to stop the 〈〉〈〈 because

Make a Rainbow Crow

Duplicate onto construction paper.   Use crayons to color the crow with many bright colors. Color thickly, so it looks and feels waxy.

Make a Rainbow Crow *(cont.)*

Crayon Scratching

1. Follow the directions on page 19 to color the Rainbow Crow.

2. Cut out crow and lay on newspaper.

3. Cover crow drawing with a thin layer of chalk dust (use the chalkboard eraser).

4. Color over the entire crow with black crayon. Start from the center and color outward like rolling cookie dough. Otherwise, the wings will tear. The picture should be entirely black.

5. With an open paper clip or a nail, scratch in the feathers. The black crayon should come off and show the bright colors below. Do this step gently so the paper doesn't tear.

   Hint: This looks great, but step five can be messy. Also, it should be done in two sessions since little hands get tired coloring that hard.

Crayon Transfer

1. Follow the directions on page 19 to color the Rainbow Crow, but color it a little past the outline.

2. Lay plain white paper on the top. You must be able to see the outline of the crow picture through the white paper.

3. Using a dull pencil, trace over the lines of the crow. You may not erase.

4. When you are finished, pull off the top sheet. The crayon will transfer where you drew the pencil lines, but it will be backwards.

5. You can do this process again and again. You just need to recolor the original crow and use new pieces of white paper.

Crayon Batik

1. Follow the directions on page 19 to color the Rainbow Crow.

2. Put the paper into a container of water. Then squeeze it into a ball.

3. Gently open the paper and lay it out smoothly on newspapers.

4. Paint over the entire picture with black tempera paint or black ink. Paint smoothly from side to side. The picture should now be entirely black.

5. Gently run water over the picture. This will take off much of the paint except where the paper was creased giving a batik effect. Lay paper on newspapers to dry.

7. Cut out crow and mount on construction paper.

   Hint: This is a very dramatic project. It needs an adult for steps 3 and 5 or it might tear. If it does just wait until it is dry and tape on the back before mounting.

Rainbow Crow Play

Introduction: After the children have heard *Rainbow Crow* several times, it is simple and rewarding to turn it into a play. The teacher can be the narrator, leaving the animal parts for the students. They will have little or no speaking to do so it can be done by children of all ages, abilities, and languages.

Preparation:

1. Create a mural for a backdrop (see page 23 for directions). This is optional depending on time and materials.

2. Have students select the animal that they wish to play. Research can be done on animals of the area to bring this into the realm of science if desired.

3. Have students make their own simple costumes from ideas given on page 22.

4. Put chants from the story on charts and practice them. If children cannot memorize or read the chants, have them "read" them with you, tape record them, and play them back as you do the play.

5. Make basic props — a firestick, snowflakes, and falling snow (see page 24).

Characters:

These characters are essential: Rainbow Crow, Great Sky Spirit, Mouse, Rabbit, Possum, Owl, Beaver, Raccoon, Skunk, Coyote.

If you have more children, they can select other animals. All animals say the chants so every child gets an opportunity to speak and act.

Costumes:

Simple costumes can be made from construction paper headbands with ears, watercolor noses and whiskers (which wash off easily), and paper tails, wings, or spots.

The pictures on page 22 can serve as ideas to create your costumes.

Rainbow Crow Play *(cont.)*

Costumes

Ears:

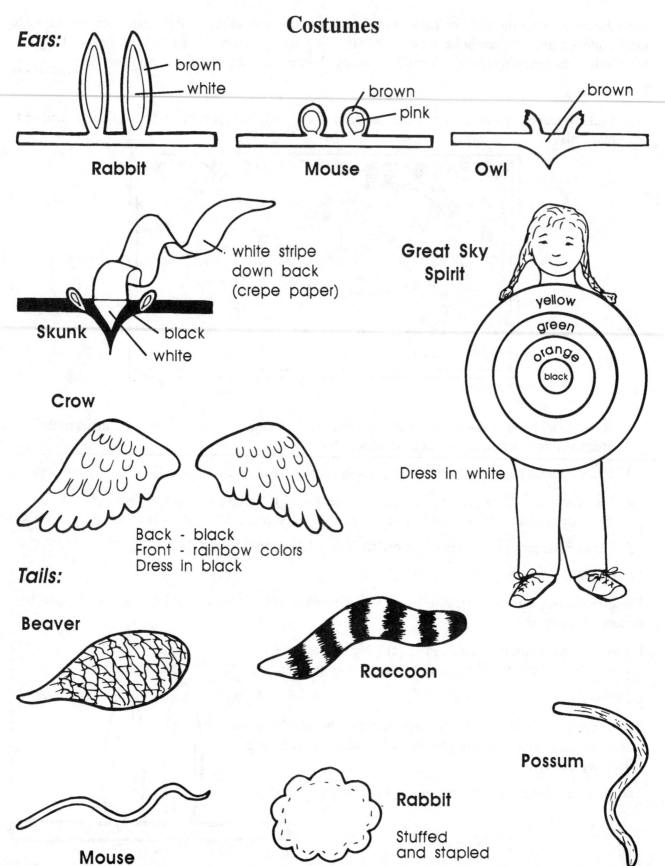

Rabbit — brown / white

Mouse — brown / pink

Owl — brown

Skunk — white stripe down back (crepe paper) — black / white

Crow — Back - black / Front - rainbow colors / Dress in black

Great Sky Spirit — yellow / green / orange / black — Dress in white

Tails:

Beaver

Raccoon

Mouse

Rabbit — Stuffed and stapled

Possum

Rainbow Crow Play *(cont.)*

Create a Woodlands Mural: This mural will be suitable for the backdrop for the Rainbow Crow play and can be displayed later as a bulletin board.

Materials: butcher paper the size of your stage area (light blue works best); colored chalk; tempera paints; various size brushes; sponges; lots of newspapers; containers for paints and water; paint smocks for the muralists; reference books for the Eastern Woodlands region

Directions:

1. Research the trees and flora of the area. Discuss types of trees for the mural.

2. Look in the *Rainbow Crow* book. Notice evergreen and deciduous trees.

3. Plan mural with the class. You can use the plan below as a starting point. Enlarge on the opaque projector and draw directly on to the butcher paper with chalk.

4. Sketch in the outline of the trees and bushes in colored chalk. Remember distance can be shown by putting large objects lower on panel and smaller objects higher; by overlapping objects; by making close objects darker and brighter, far objects lighter and grayer.

5. Fill in foreground first leaving the sky for last.

6. Outline centers of interest with paint for emphasis. After mural is complete and dry, fill in sky with side of chalk. If the entire paper is painted, it will tend to crack when moved.

    Hints: So more people can work at a time, cut mural into sections and set up several painting areas. To fill in large sections quickly, use sponges rather than brushes.

Rainbow Crow Play *(cont.)*

Props:

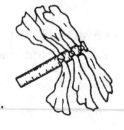

Firestick: Ruler tied with yellow, red, orange crepe paper

Snowflakes: Mount snowflakes from page 14 on rulers. As animal is covered with snow child holds flake in front of face.

Falling snow: Take a long sheet of white butcher paper. Cut lengthwise like snow drifts and roll up. As the story unfolds, so does the snow. Have two students in charge, one on either side. Then as the crow flies around melting the snow the children roll up the snowdrift and take it off stage.

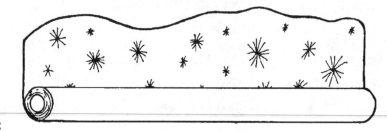

Staging the Play:

With mural in the background, have other animals scattered around the stage. Rainbow Crow should stand on a chair in front of a mural tree. Snowdrift should be rolled up at the front of the stage.

Narrator reads and animals pantomime actions . . ."Long, long ago, before the Two-Legged walked the Earth, the weather was always warm and the animals were always happy."

If students are reading, copy pages from the book and highlight their parts. For example:

Possum: ``. . . Owl is the wisest. Perhaps he should go . . .''

All: (whispering) ``But no.... He might get lost in the light of day. So owl should not go.''

Beaver: ``Perhaps Raccoon should go.'' etc.

The Legend of the Bluebonnet

retold by Tomie de Paola

Summary

This Comanche legend from the Texas region describes a tribe which has been experiencing a drought for a long time. The Great Spirit has told the Shaman that the tribe's most precious possession must be sacrificed to bring rain. A young girl named She-Who-Is-Alone knows that sacrificing her doll will save the tribe. This doll is all that she has left of her parents and her ancestors. However, she is unselfish. The doll is sacrificed. The life giving rains come, leaving a field of Bluebonnets in memory of her offering.

Sample Plan

The Week Before Day I

- Pick flowers, weeds, and leaves for Nature's Window art project to be done at the end of the unit. Begin pressing them. This process will take about ten days. (See page 35)

Day I

- Daily Writing Activities: Give yourself a Native American name (page 26)
- Learn about the Great Basin
- Great Spirits - Part I (page 28)
- Great Spirits - Part II (page 29)

Day II

- Share predictions from Great Spirits - Part II paper
- Read aloud the first part of the book to page 13
- For review, write the first part of the story in Native American symbols (see page 34)
- Do She-Who-Is-Alone's doll (page 30)
- Homework: Your Favorite Possession (page 30)

Day III

- Share favorite possession papers and things
- Read aloud the end of the story
- Write the ending of the story in Native American symbols (page 34)
- Make a Skin Story (page 32)

Day IV

- Lupine art project- fingerprints (page 27)
- In co-op groups, write sections of story on animal "skins"
- Share sections with the total class

Day V

- Bind Skin Stories into a Big Book
- Do rain dance (page 36)
- Read *Legend of the Indian Paintbrush*. See Bibliography, page 80
- Discuss both legends. Do Venn Diagram (page 31)
- Divide into small groups based on the flowers brought in
- Write legend in Native American symbols
- Divide up Native American symbol story written as a class
- Make into a Big Book

Overview of Activities

Preparation: As part of a science lesson, have the students pick flowers, weeds, and leaves and press them. Directions for this activity, Nature's Window, are on page 35. This project is done after reading the book. Pressing the flowers takes at least 10 days.

SETTING THE STAGE

1. Discuss the Great Desert Basin area. The Comanche are a major tribe of this area. Have reference materials available for students to look at.

2. Add Comanche to the wall chart. They were known for their prowess with horses but they lived in an inhospitable area. They ate what they could find or hunt: roots, berries, snakes, lizards, rabbits. They did not farm. The tribes in this area were often on the verge of starvation. They lived in tepees as depicted in the story.

3. Have the students add this information to their own Native American Reference Chart (page 75) using either words or pictures.

4. Have students make drought symbols with their names (see page 34, Picture Dictionary) to use for attendance graphing. Do Attendance Graphing question #1 under *The Legend of the Bluebonnet* and discuss (page 47).

5. Have the students give themselves a Native American name. Explain to them that the girl in the story had lost her parents and the other members of her family. She was called She-Who-Is-Alone. At the end of the story she will get a new name based on what she does. Give some examples to get them started: She-Who-Teaches-Children, He-Who-Chases-Rabbits, She-Who-Swims-Like-a-Duck. Have the students illustrate their names and share them.

6. Have the students make rattles from musical instrument section (page 68).

7. Have them use their instruments while you read the instructions from Great Spirits – Part 1 (page 28). Then have them brainstorm what they think the book is about. Working in pairs, have the students finish the paper. Share the predictions with the class.

8. Use Great Spirits – Part 2 to have the children predict what the Great Spirits will ask of the Comanche people. This could be done as a total group on a chart as well.

ENJOYING THE BOOK

1. Read the first half of the book to the class.

2. Compare the predictions from Great Spirits – Part II with the book.

3. As a class write the first part of the book using Native American Picture Symbols. Be sure that the students know that picture stories use basically nouns and verbs. The rest of the words that we use in writing are left out.

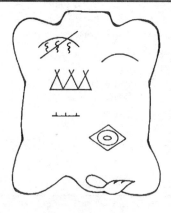

There was no rain. The village was dying from the drought. They asked Great Spirit what to do.

Overview of Activities (cont.)

ENJOYING THE BOOK (cont.)

4. Have the students make She-Who-Is-Alone's most precious possession. Reread the section of the story that describes the doll. List the attributes of the doll if necessary. Use page 30. Assign homework: students take the paper home and draw their most precious possession on the other side.

5. Share homework. Do Venn diagram comparing your precious possession with She-Who-Is Alone's doll (page 31).

6. Read aloud to the end of the story.

7. Review the story with the class using Native American symbols on a chart or chalkboard to help them remember the key events and sequence.

8. Have them work in pairs using the skin outline from page 33 to summarize a part of the story. They can pick their favorite part or you can assign each pair a section to do.

9. Have each pair write or dictate their skin story and share with the group.

10. Order the sections of the story sequentially.

EXTENDING THE BOOK

1. Make a Big Book. Have the students make animal skins. See complete directions on page 32.

   Have each pair (from #8 above) transfer their section of the story onto the animal skin. Use extra skins to add to the story when necessary.

   Mount skins on large butcher paper. Have the pairs write their section of the story in words below their skin.

   Bind the skins into a Big Book.

   Keep the book in the class library, share with other classes, donate the book to the school library, or display each page on a bulletin board or clothesline.

2. Do the Rain Dance on page 36.

3. Make lupines (another name for bluebonnets) using fingerprint printing technique. Cut them out and make a field of lupines as a background for displayed skin stories.

4. Read *The Legend of the Indian Paintbrush* (see Bibliography, page 80) and compare and contrast the stories.

5. Make Nature's Window from the pressed flowers collected during preparation. See page 35 for directions.

6. Create a legend to explain your flower.

7. Write the legend in symbols.

8. Study wildflowers. Have pictures of various flowers and have the children make up names for them and give their reasons.

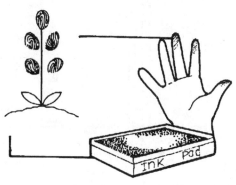

Name _____

Great Spirits – Part 1

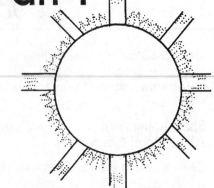

'' 'Great Spirits,

the land is dying. Your People are dying, too,'

the long line of dancers sang.

'Tell us what we have done to anger you . . .' ''

These are the first four lines of the book, *The Legend of the Bluebonnet,* that you are going to be experiencing. On the lines below **predict** what you think the book will be about.

_____

_____

_____

_____

_____

_____

_____

_____

_____

Name _____

Great Spirits – Part 2

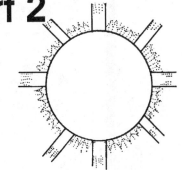

" 'End this drought. Save your People.
Tell us what we must do so you will send the rain
that will bring back life.' "

On the lines below, **predict** what you think the
Great Spirits will ask of the Comanche people.

_____

_____

_____

_____

_____

_____

_____

_____

_____

_____

Name _____

Precious Possessions

Mine

She-Who-Is-Alone's

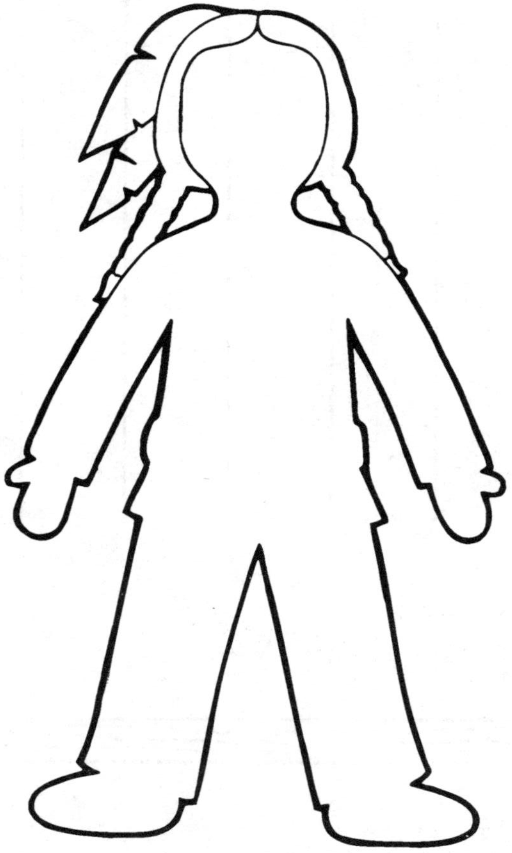

*See page 27 for directions.

30

Name _____

Likenesses and Differences

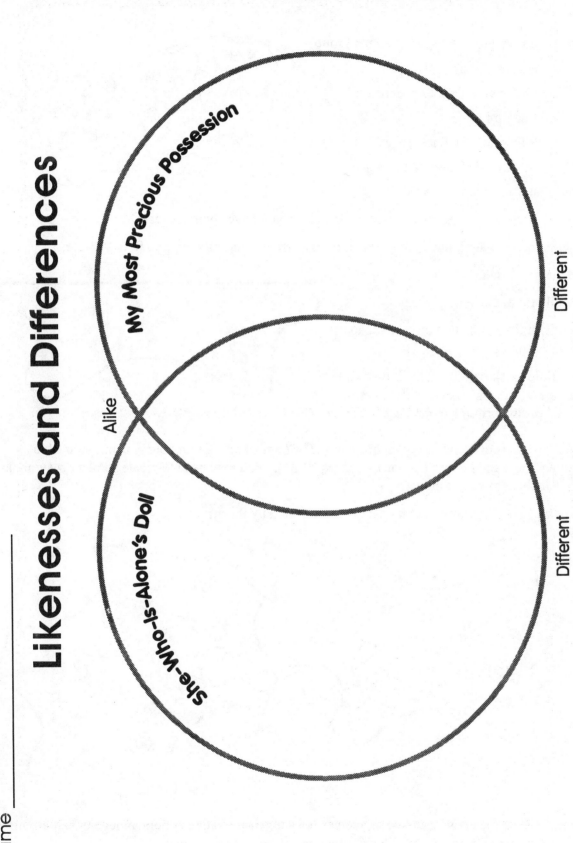

My Most Precious Possession

She-Who-Is-Alone's Doll

Alike

Different

Different

Cut out Venn diagram. Glue the doll and possession pictures from page 30 and Venn diagram onto a sheet of large paper. At the bottom write about your possession. Tell why it is precious to you.

Make a Skin Story

Materials: brown grocery bag (½ bag per group)

bucket or sink of water

brown and black tempera paint

fine tip felt pens

Skin Planning Sheet (page 33)

Picture Dictionary (page 34)

Directions: Make an "animal" skin

1. Cut out bottom and seam of bag; then cut in half so you have about a square.

2. Crumple the bag; dip it in water; squeeze; remove from water; uncrumple. Repeat twice.

3. Fold the paper in half.

4. Carefully rip out an animal shape.

5. Carefully unfold and lay it on a newspaper with any printing up.

6. Mix a little black paint with the brown and paint one side of the "skin" while it is still wet. Cover the printing on the bag.

7. When "skin" is dry, "write" your section of *The Legend of the Bluebonnet* using your Skin Planning Sheet and Picture Dictionary (pages 33-34). You may need to create some new symbols. If so, add them to your dictionary.

The story should follow a circular pattern as indicated by the arrows.

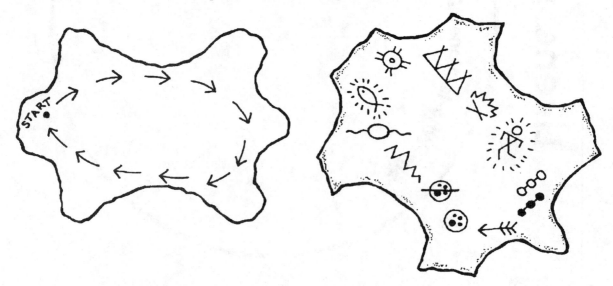

Extension: Redo the activity and write another (or your own) Native American legend explaining the origin of your flower. This can be done as homework.

Make a Skin Story *(cont.)*

Skin Planning Sheet

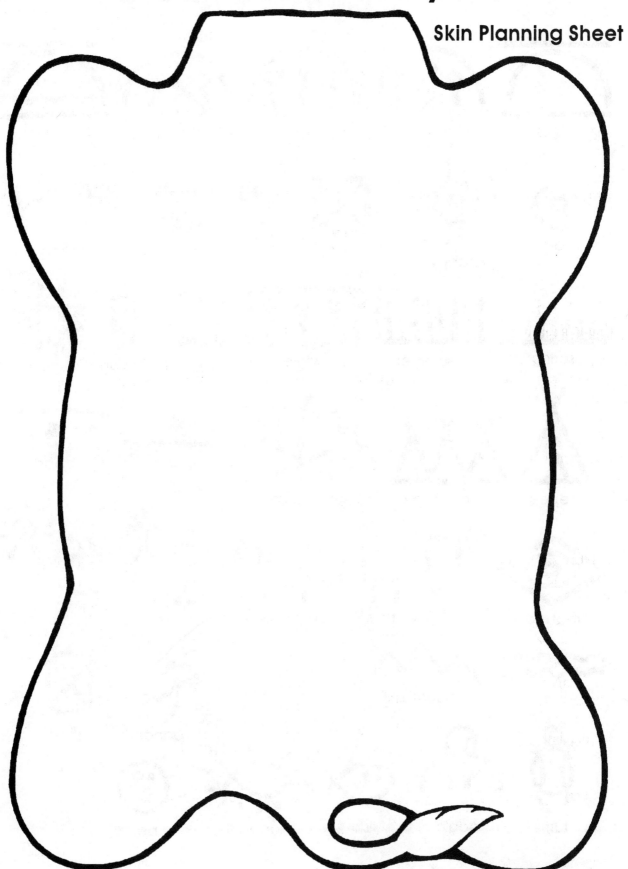

Picture Dictionary

clear weather   rain   snow   no rain   storm

sad   happy   help   war   peace

spring   summer   winter   sun   moon   star

tepee   Indian camp   campfire   good   bad

Great Spirit   horse   horse tracks   man   woman   boy   girl   wise

river   mountains   lake   dancer   drum

turtle   eagle   fish   many fish   bear

Nature's Window

In *The Legend of the Bluebonnet* the origin of the fields of lupines are explained. In this art project you will discover the beauty of the wildflowers and "weeds" in your area.

Materials: (per person)   2 pieces of waxed paper (9" X 12"/22.5 X 30cm)

scissors; stapler; hole punch

dried leaves, weeds, flowers (pressed)

scraps of colored tissue paper

white glue

newspapers

iron

2 construction paper strips (2" X 9"/5 X 22.5cm)

one 18"/45cm piece of string or yarn

Directions:

1. Collect and press leaves and flowers in a heavy book. It will take at least a week for them to dry.

2. Lay out one piece of waxed paper. Arrange dried leaves, flowers, and pieces of tissue paper.

3. When you have a pleasing pattern, glue them down with small dabs of white glue.

4. Place this piece of wax paper, design side up, on top of several sheets of newspaper. Lay a second sheet of wax paper on top.

5. With iron set on low, iron over the wax paper, moving the iron from the center outward. The two pieces of wax paper will melt together.

   Hint: Test the iron first before using it on children's projects. If it is too hot, the paper will stick to the iron. For insurance, put a sheet of newspaper over the top before ironing.

6. Fold construction paper strips in half lengthwise. Staple them to the top and bottom of the "window."

7. Punch a hole at each end of the top strip. Attach the string or yarn.

8. Hang in a window so the light shines through it.

Extension: Create your own Native American legend of your flower's origin.

Creating a Rain Dance

Native Americans held many ceremonies designed to make sure they had the food they needed to **survive**. These ceremonies almost always included music and rhythmic movement or dance. Singing and **chanting** were done to the rhythm of handcrafted rattles, drums, rasps, flutes, and/or whistles.

Rain was essential to the farming tribes for their crops and the hunting tribes for the health of the animals they used for food. So, rain dances were often performed in time of drought.

Your whole class can participate in this activity. Besides improving listening skills, this movement activity encourages concentration and awareness of others.

Directions

1. Students stand in a circle. Everyone must be still and quiet.

2. The leader (either a student or the teacher) begins by rubbing his thumb and two **fingers back and** forth to make the "mist."

3. He turns toward the person on his right, who then begins rubbing his thumb and two **fingers.**

4. Each person "passes the mist" until all children are making the mist.

5. The leader then changes his motion to rubbing his palms back and forth. He "**passes the drizzle**" to the student on his right and so on until all children are making drizzle.

6. The process continues with "rain" — patting thighs; "downpour" — stomping feet.

7. To end the storm, the process is reversed until the leader is making the mist alone.

mist   **drizzle**   **rain**   **downpour**

Extensions: Add rhythms with instruments made by children. (See directions, pages 67-68.)

Add a rain chant created by the class.

Writing Poems

Color Poem

Use after completing *Arrow to the Sun*. Refer students to illustrations of the Pot Maker from the story.

Materials: colored chalk; a copy of pages 38 and 39; facial tissue; scissors; glue

Directions: Using only one color of chalk, color your pot with variations of that color. Some sections should be dark, some light. Use the tissue to lighten some sections. Cut out the pot and glue to the top of a 12" X 18" (30 X 45cm) piece of construction paper. Use the Color Poem page to write or dictate your poem.

Example:

Purple

Fields of flowers

Moving with the breeze

Spreading their fragrance

Purple

Rainbow Poem Book

Suggested for use after *Rainbow Crow*. Discuss when rainbows appear.

Materials: watercolors or crayons; a copy of page 40 per person; 4 copies of page 41 per person; 6 sheets of 9" X 12" colored construction paper; scissors; glue; stapler

Directions: Make a cover for a Rainbow Poem Book. (See page 40 for directions.) Write a poem for each color on your rainbow book cover. Use the following pattern: Title: color name; First line: 3 things of that color; Second line: Complete "Makes me feel . . ."; Third line: Repeat color name. (Use page 41.)

Example:

Red

Apple, flag stripe, heart

Makes me feel happy

Red

Sensory Poem

Use anytime during the unit. Students need to have experience with Native American symbols (page 34). Provide a copy of page 42 per person.

Directions: Discuss things in nature that you might see, hear, touch, taste, and smell. Give examples of colorful phrases rather than single word responses. Have students visualize a favorite place in nature before writing. After writing the five phrases, design an appropriate Native American symbol to fill in the box.

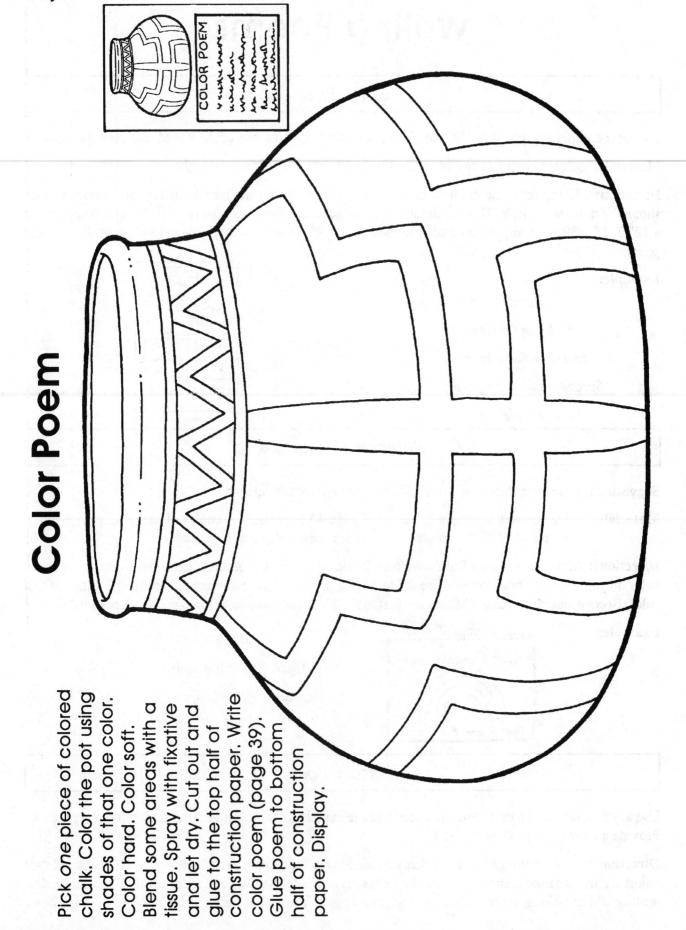

Color Poem

Pick one piece of colored chalk. Color the pot using shades of that one color. Color hard. Color soft. Blend some areas with a tissue. Spray with fixative and let dry. Cut out and glue to the top half of construction paper. Write color poem (page 39). Glue poem to bottom half of construction paper. Display.

38

Color Poem

1. Name your color:

2. Name something in nature of that color:

3. Tell something about the object on line #2:

4. Tell another thing about the thing on line #2:

5. Name your color:

Rainbow Poem Book Cover

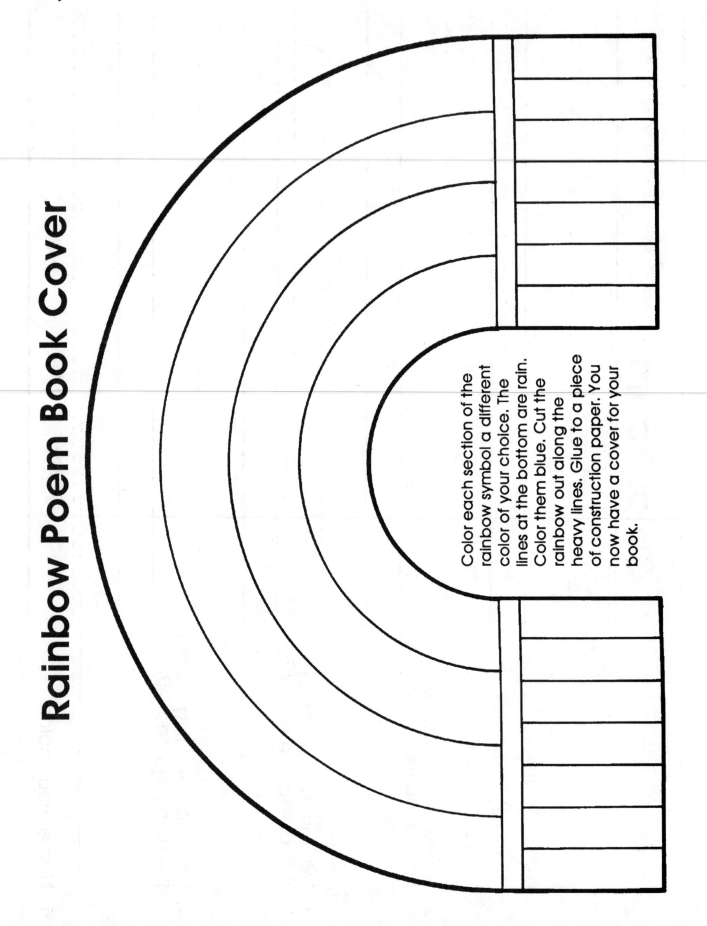

Color each section of the rainbow symbol a different color of your choice. The lines at the bottom are rain. Color them blue. Cut the rainbow out along the heavy lines. Glue to a piece of construction paper. You now have a cover for your book.

(Color name.)

(Three things that are that color.)

Makes me feel

(Complete the phrase.)

(Repeat color name.)

Sensory Poem

Native American songs and stories are usually about nature. Complete the following sentences with phrases about things from nature. Create a Native American-type symbol for each. Draw it in the box.

I like to see . . .

I like to hear . . .

I like to touch . . .

I like to taste . . .

I like to smell . . .

Attendance Graphing

This is a unique and relatively easy method of combining a math activity with reading/language arts while having students work both individually and in cooperative groups. It takes from 15 to 30 minutes per day.

First, make a name tag for each child in the class. While reading *Arrow to the Sun*, use a sun pattern. While reading *The Legend of the Bluebonnet*, use a drought symbol. As you read *Rainbow Crow*, use a rainbow symbol. If you have magnetic chalkboards, attach a magnetic strip to the back of each name tag. These strips can be purchased at a craft store. They can be easily cut with a pair of scissors and have a sticky side so they adhere to the back of the student's tag. If you do not have magnetic boards, you can use double-faced tape.

Second, display one of the questions from page 46 each day either on the chalkboard or another convenient place. As the children enter the room, they use their tag to answer the question before they take their seats—thus, the term "attendance graphing." The absent students' tags will remain in a holding zone. See example:

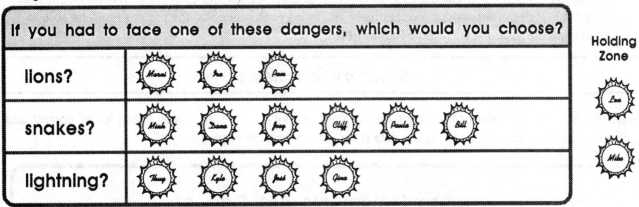

Third, as the students take their seats, they take out their journals. They write down the question and their response. Then they write at least three reasons for their choice. Those that finish early can do an illustration. (While the students do this, you can take roll, collect homework, and do other basic chores.)

Group Talk-Around

In groups of three to five, students take turns reading their journal entries. There are three rules for this that should be posted on a chart.

Group Talk-Around Rules

1. Only one person speaks at a time.
2. Everyone has eye contact with the speaker.
3. Each person has a turn and must speak loudly enough for every person in the group to hear.

Doing this daily gives students practice in writing, listening, and speaking. It also gives children a chance to know one another better and fosters a feeling of class unity.

Attendance Graphing (cont.)

During Math Period

Students can work in cooperative groups using this round table technique to write or say **summary** statements (see below). After the initial training, this should take about 5 to 8 minutes.

1. Students should be arranged in groups of four to five. Use the same groups that were used for the Group Talk-Around, if possible.

2. Give only one piece of paper and one pencil to each group.

3. Have the students use the attendance graphing information on the board to make true **mathematical** statements. One child writes his/her statement, then hands the paper and the pencil to the student on the right. The next student writes another statement on the paper and passes the paper and pencil to the right. This continues around the table until the teacher calls time. (Allow about four minutes.) If the group works cooperatively and helps each other out, the paper should be able to go around the group at least three to four times.

Summary Statements

Summary Statements need to be taught for the math activity. Here are some examples of correct and incorrect summary statements using the data from the example on page 43.

These Statements Are Correct

Four chose lightning.
More chose snakes than lightning.
The smallest number chose lions.

These Statements Are Not Correct

Dana is afraid of lions.
José doesn't like snakes.
I would be afraid of anything.

4. Once time has been called, have the groups total their responses. The group with the **greatest** number of responses gets to share their paper with the class. The rest of the class must decide whether the responses are mathematically correct.

5. Have the group with the greatest number of correct responses tell the rest of the class how they worked cooperatively to do such a good job.

6. Use the multipurpose graph (page 45) to make a bar graph of your results.

Bar Graph

Title: _____

	16				
	15				
	14				
	13				
	12				
	11				
	10				
	9				
	8				
	7				
	6				
	5				
	4				
	3				
	2				
	1				
Choices					

Directions:

1. Put title on graph.

2. Put choices at the bottom.

3. Count responses on class graph.

4. Color in the correct amount for each choice.

5. Be sure each bar starts at the double line and goes up to the correct number.

Daily Writing Topics

These topics can be used for attendance graphing (see page 43-44) and/or written language activities.

Use with *Arrow to the Sun*

1. If you were a Pueblo Native American, which job would you prefer? Tell why.

   corn planter   **pottery maker**   **arrow maker**

2. Which do you think would be the most frightening? Explain.

   a room full of snakes   **a room full of lions**   **a room full of lightning**

3. In the story the Boy became an arrow and traveled to the sun. If you could become an arrow and be shot somewhere, which area would you prefer? Tell why.

   the mountains   **the beach**   **the moon**

4. In the story the Boy was filled with the power of the sun. He had to return to earth and bring his spirit to the world of men. If you could bring a gift to the world, which would it be?

   everlasting peace   **end hunger**   **more money**

   (The last two topics could be done several times with the students suggesting the categories.)

Use with *Rainbow Crow*

1. Which is your favorite color? Tell why you like it.

   red   **blue**   **yellow**

   (This can be done with other colors or expanded to more than three categories.)

2. In the story, many animals want to help stop the snow. Which animals do you think could best do the job? Tell what your choice might do.

   owl   **raccoon**   **coyote**

3. The animals in the story had never seen snow. Have you seen snow? Tell about a favorite time in the snow.

   often   **occasionally**   **never**

4. Which climate would you rather live in? Give three reasons for your choice.

   very, very warm   **very, very cold**

5. If the crow knew ahead of time that he would become ugly and lose his beautiful voice, do you think he would have gone?

   yes   **no**

6. If you would become ugly and lose your voice, would you go?

   yes   **no**

Daily Writing Topics *(cont.)*

Use with *The Legend of the Bluebonnet*

1. In the story, the tribe experiences a drought. Which do you think would be worse? Tell why.

   a drought   **a flood**

2. She-Who-Is-Alone sacrificed her doll to save the tribe. Would you do the same with your most precious possession?

   yes   **no**   **not sure**

4. She-Who-Is-Alone got a new name, She-Who-Dearly-Loved-Her-People. If you could have a new name, which word might it include? Tell why that word is like you.

   brave   **smart**   **funny**

5. At the end of the story, fields of wild flowers appeared. Which is your favorite flower?

   rose   **daisy**   **orchid**

(All topics in this section can be used several times with the students suggesting the categories.)

Homework — The Home/School Connection

Most all of these topics can be used for homework. Each child can go home and interview their parents and report their findings back to the class orally, in writing, or group graph as appropriate. This helps to carry the literature into the home and helps students to discuss some of the issues from the books.

Other Non-Graphing Journal Topics

(Use any time during the unit.)

1. Draw the main character from the story. Tell how that character is like you.

2. Tell how the main character is different from you.

3. Draw a favorite scene from a book and tell why you like it. Draw the most exciting scene, the funniest scene, the scariest scene, etc.

4. Make a Venn diagram to compare the books. Tell how they are alike. Tell how they are different.

5. Copy a sentence that makes you happy or sad. Explain why.

6. After hearing all three books, tell which one you liked the best. Explain your choice.

7. Design a new book jacket for one of the books. Tell why your picture represents the book.

8. Write letters to characters in the books and tell them about yourself.

9. If you could be a character in the book, which one would you be and why?

10. Create your own ideas.

Tell and Draw Stories

Directions to the teacher-storyteller:

As you tell the stories, draw each part on a chalkboard. You may wish to simplify or expand on the stories. Children love to hear them over and over again, and tell them to each other.

After the children are familiar with a story, provide a mini-chalkboard to allow the students to become the storyteller. Hopefully the children will add to and embellish the story with each retelling.

The Big Fish

It was a bright, spring morning...two young Native American braves sat beside a lake. "Let's go fishing!" they said. So they climbed into their canoe that looked like this . . .

They paddled and paddled in their little canoe. They sailed east and they sailed west. They sailed north and they sailed south. But... they didn't see one single fish! Quite suddenly they heard a big SPLASH. An enormous fish popped its head out of the water like this . . .

The fish had gobbled up the bait the young brave had put on his fishing line. He started swimming away very fast. The big fish was so strong that he dragged the braves and the canoe all around the lake. It was an exciting but frightening ride . . .

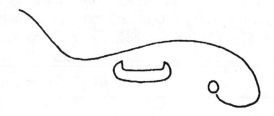

They even went down a waterfall just like this . . .

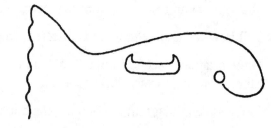

Finally the fish began to tire. It swam slower and slower and slower. (Draw the line back from the "waterfall" slower as you tell this part.) He swam very close to the canoe. Oh my, but he was a big fish!

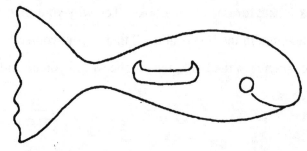

48

Tell and Draw Stories *(cont.)*

Two Little Native Americans

Once there were two little Native American boys. They lived in two cozy tepees with their families. One stood here . . . and one stood here . . .

They lived beside a big lake. This is the lake.

Now this is a very strange lake. Most lakes are surrounded by trees but this lake had only two rather small trees that grew on the opposite side of the lake right here . . .

In the middle of the lake there were two islands exactly the same size . . .

One day the two Native American boys decided it was time to prove to the elders of the tribe that they were old enough to be considered men. Their plan was to camp out overnight on the nearest island. Well, they took their canoe and, without telling anyone, paddled off to the island like this . . .

When they arrived on the island, they set up their camp right here . . . They started a campfire and then settled down for the night. But all of a sudden, they heard a strange noise. It went OOOOOOOOOOOOO.

This frightened them very much indeed. They ran to their canoe and paddled quickly to the other island. And they landed right here.... And this is where they built another campfire. Soon, however, they became very sleepy because of all the excitement. They tried to stay awake, but they couldn't keep their eyes open and they were soon fast asleep. Suddenly they heard the strange sound again — louder this time! OOOOOOOOOOOOOOOOOOOOO!!!!!!!

This noise frightened the two boys so much that they jumped in the water and swam to the edge of the lake. They realized that they were not yet ready to be men. They were very happy to return to their cozy tepees. What was it that frightened the boys? A LARGE OWL!

Name _____

Pottery Geometry

Native Americans decorated their clothes, pots, toys, and other belongings. They often drew geometric designs using dyes from plants. These designs were patterns made of triangles, squares, rectangles, and many other shapes.

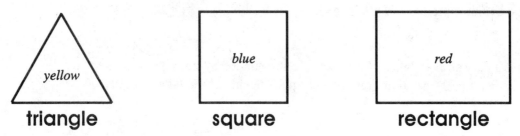

| triangle | square | rectangle |

Find the geometric shapes used to decorate the pot below. Color the triangles yellow. Color the squares blue. Color the rectangles red.

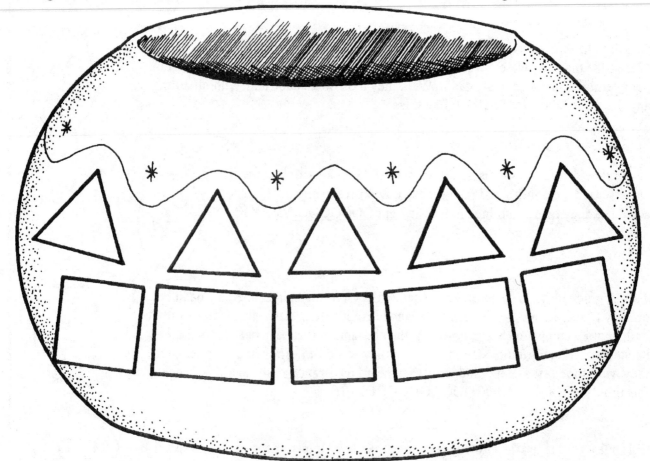

Challenge: Make your own geometric design. What other shapes can you use?

Picture Problems

Count the Native American symbols in each group and write the number below it. Look closely at the math sign. Solve the problem.

	Turtles		Bears
3 + 2 = 5		___ + ___ = ___	

	Drums		Tepees
___ − ___ = ___		___ − ___ = ___	

	Dancers		Stars
___ + ___ = ___		___ + ___ = ___	

	Suns		Fish
___ − ___ = ___		___ − ___ = ___	

Create some of your own problems using other symbols from the Picture Dictionary, page 34.

Growing Corn

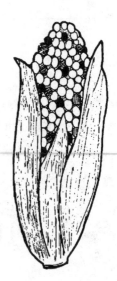

Corn, also called maize, was first found in North America. The Native Americans began collecting it and using it for food almost 10,000 years ago. From that time on the use of corn has increased so much that it is now one of the world's most important crops.

For this activity you are going to plant and grow your own corn.

Materials: 2 or 3 corn seeds per student; clear plastic cups; soil; water

Directions: Fill a clear, plastic cup with soil halfway to the top. Plant 2 or 3 corn seeds near the sides of the glass and cover with soil. Water the seeds, until the soil is moist (like a wrung out washcloth). Continue to keep moist, but not soggy. Give full sunlight. When the plants reach 6" tall they may be transplanted to the ground.

On the chart below draw what your plant looks like as it grows.

Week 1	Week 2
Week 3	Week 4

What did you learn? _____

_____

52

Nature Hike

Native Americans had a special bond to the earth. They appreciated the food and building materials that the earth gave them. The Native Americans respected the earth and described it in detail in their songs and stories demonstrating the importance of it in their lives.

See if you can appreciate the earth as much as the Native Americans did. Go on a nature hike in your school yard or park with your class. Be very quiet so you can hear the many sounds around you and not disturb any animals that you may see. Write down what you see, hear, smell, and touch on the chart below.

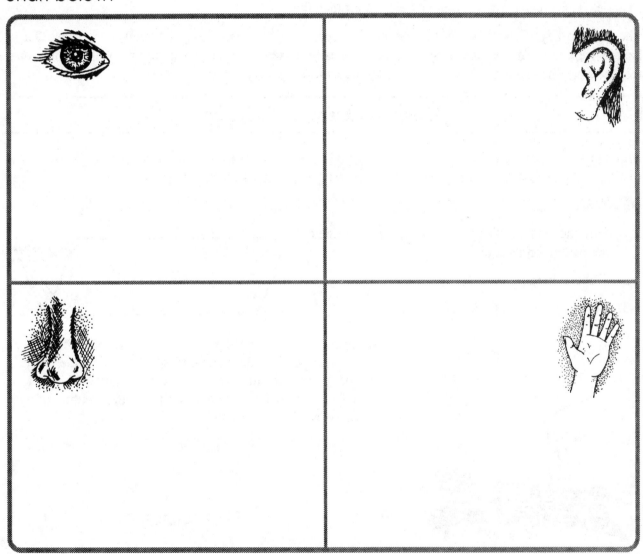

Challenge: Write a story or song about what you saw, heard, smelled, and touched on your nature hike. Share your story or song with the class.

Canoes of the Native Americans

Most Native American tribes traveled primarily by foot or by horse. However, those located by lakes, rivers, and oceans designed variations of canoes for transportation.

One such boat was called the dugout. It was used by the tribes of the plateau. With only stone tools and hot coals they constructed a canoe from a long length of tree trunk. A part of one side was chopped flat, coals were applied, and a hollow was carefully burned into the log. The heat of the coals drove the moist sap into the unburned portions of the log making the rest of the log more water resistant. Then the ends were chopped and burned into rough points. The completed dugout was long and narrow and moved easily through the water.

Another type of canoe was built by the tribes of the Woodlands. They designed a frame of wood or animal bones and covered it with birchbark which grew plentifully. The bark from a single large tree could cover a canoe. This created a much lighter weight craft than the dugout.

The Eskimo kayak also has this frame-type construction. However, it was covered with hides. These kayaks were much more seaworthy than the dugouts because they could bend with the waves rather than resist them. Therefore, the hunting area of the people was greatly increased.

Making a "Birchbark" Canoe

Materials: 1 canoe pattern per student (page 55); 1 piece of tan construction paper 12" X 18" (30 X 45cm) per student; crayons; scissors; glue; string; stapler

Directions:

1. Fold the tan paper lengthwise. Place the flat side of the pattern on its fold.

2. Trace around pattern.

3. Cut out except on folded edge.

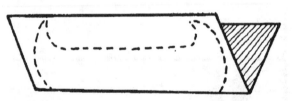

4. Open the canoe and attach strips of string, which have been dipped into thinned white glue, to the inside from end to end and side to side to create a frame-like effect. This is optional, but it increases the understanding of the canoe's original construction.

5. When the glue dries, staple or glue the ends together.

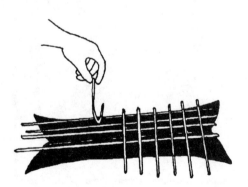

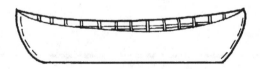

6. Add a paddle, paddler, and create a lake or stream to finish off the project.

Canoe Pattern

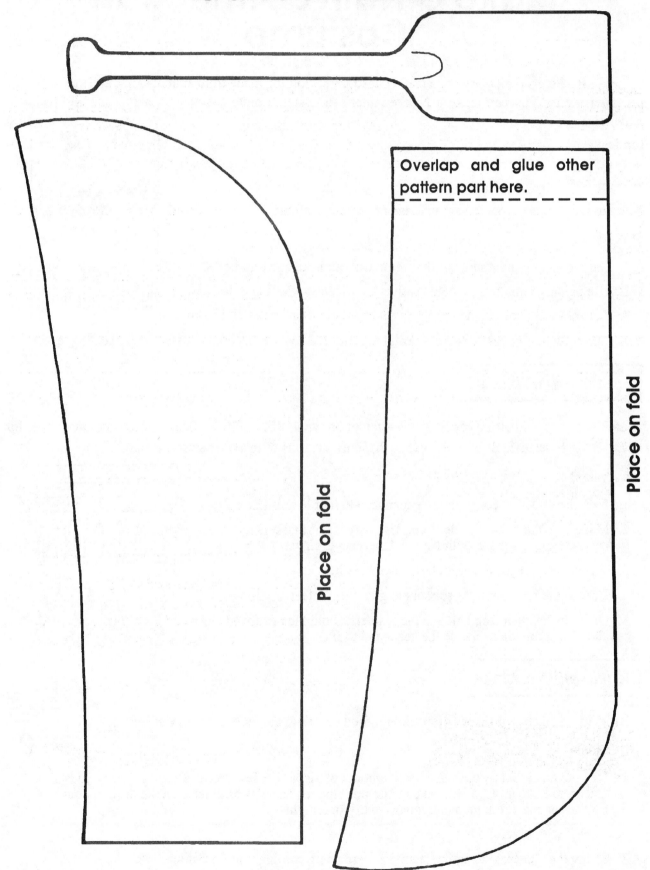

Overlap and glue other pattern part here.

Place on fold

Place on fold

Make a Native American Costume

Tribes of the Plains typically wore a feather headdress, clothing made from animal skins, and necklaces for ornamentation. You can make a Native American costume quite easily with a few readily available materials.

Vest

Materials: large grocery bag; markers or paints; scissors

Directions

1. Cut the bag up the middle of the front. Cut out head and arm holes.
2. Use paints or markers to make Native American symbols and designs.
3. Cut fringe at the bottom.
4. Carefully put on vest. (You may want to reinforce weak areas on the inside with masking tape.)

Feather Headband

Materials: construction paper strips — tan or brown 4" X 24" (10 X 60cm), various colored paper for feathers 2 ½" X 9"(6.25 X 22.5cm); crayons or markers; scissors; stapler; glue

Directions:

1. Fold the 4" X 24" construction paper strip in half lengthwise.
2. Make sure the opening side is up. Use crayons or markers to decorate the headband with Native American designs.
3. Trace a feather pattern to make as many feathers as you wish.
4. Cut out the feathers. Use scissors to give them a feathery look.
5. Open the headband and glue in the feathers. Fold the headband and glue it together. Staple the headband to fit.

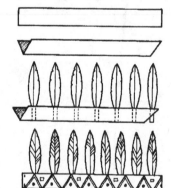

Macaroni Necklace

Materials: different shapes of macaroni; food coloring; alcohol; jar; heavy string

Directions:

1. Dye the macaroni by putting a small amount of alcohol, a few drops of food coloring, and macaroni in a jar. Gently shake the jar until the macaroni is brighter than the desired color. Spread the macaroni on paper towels to dry overnight.
2. Repeat with several other colors.
3. String the macaroni in an interesting pattern using cotton string or fishing line.

56

Totem Poles

Totem poles were only made by the tribes of the Northwest. Contrary to popular belief, they have no religious meaning; they tell a story. Strangely enough, if the onlooker does not already know the story, he cannot ''read'' the pole. There are many totems today that have lost their stories. These are called puzzle poles. A totem pole was a symbol of the family's or chief's importance. The taller the totem, the more important the individual. A pole was erected for various reasons, usually at a big party called a Potlatch. Preserving the poles was almost impossible. They were left outside to endure the sun, wind, and rain. Therefore, they were painted with brightly colored animal oils that decorated as well as preserved.

Of the more than 100 symbols carved on the wooden poles, some were used more than others. Tribes often selected animals to identify with. Birds were popular. Snakes symbolized evil. Halibut, frogs, beavers, bears, killer whales, seals, and thunderbirds were also often used. To save space animals were often represented by parts rather than the whole.

Color The Land of the Totems map below to see where the different tribes that created totem poles lived.

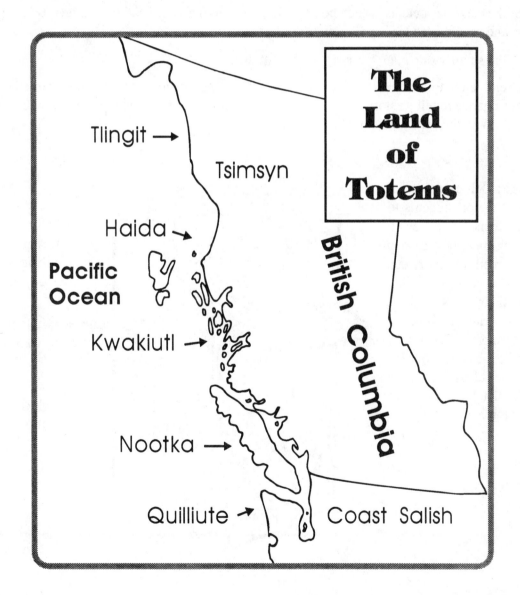

Totem Poles *(cont.)*

Since totems were used to tell a story, this project is to be done by the entire class. It can be used to build class unity and identity.

Building a Class Totem

Materials: lots of boxes; construction paper; stapler; scissors; paints and brushes; lots of newspaper; pictures of totem poles

Directions:

1. As a class, list certain special events such as a class field trip or a special visitor, etc. The longer the list the better.

2. Stack the boxes in an interesting manner. Use the stacking pattern to plan the totem.

3. Once the class has decided which box should represent which special class event, take the boxes apart and assign each to a small group.

4. Have the small group plan, "carve," and paint their section. Dry.

5. Reassemble the totem. Have your own class Potlatch. A Potlatch was a ceremony to erect a totem pole, a chance to tell its story, and a reason to have a party. Have each group tell their part of the story. Invite the principal, parents, and others.

Homework: An extension of this project is for students to construct their own small totems using small boxes, soup cans, construction paper, etc. These should represent milestones in their lives such as learning to ride a bike or playing a sport. Then they should write the stories of their totems. The class can have another Potlatch to celebrate these new totems.

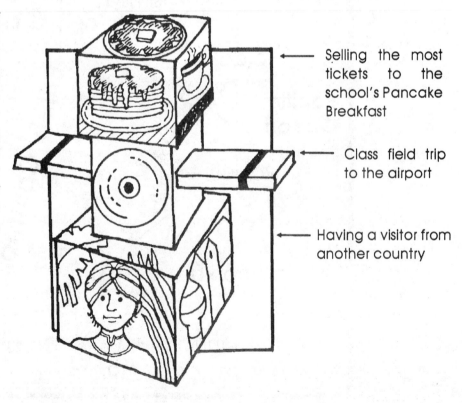

Selling the most tickets to the school's Pancake Breakfast

Class field trip to the airport

Having a visitor from another country

Sand Painting

Sand painting was practiced by many of the tribes of the American Southwest. It probably began with the Pueblo Native Americans. Originally, it was practiced only as a part of a healing ceremony conducted by medicine men. The patient was placed in the center of the painting while chants were sung. A rattle made from a dried gourd was used by the medicine man as he chanted. During the ceremony certain parts of the painting were rubbed on the patient's body. At the end of the healing ceremony, the painting was destroyed; thus destroying the patient's illness.

Fortunately, sand paintings are now done on boards and saved so we can enjoy this beautiful art form. Here is an easy and enjoyable way for children to experience this activity.

Materials: containers of salt (have the children bring them in)

colored chalk

paper plates and ample newspaper

white glue with a good dispenser top

9" X 12" (22.5 X 30cm) piece of cardboard

design from page 60, if desired

Directions:

1. Prepare your sand painting board. Use the sun design on page 60 or invent a design of your own and draw it on a piece of paper. Glue the paper to your board (cardboard). Be sure the glue is completely dry before you go on.

2. This is best done outdoors. Prepare the area. Lay down newspaper. Set out a paper plate for each color to be used.

3. Demonstrate salt coloring technique. Put 2-3 tablespoons of salt onto a plate. Select a piece of colored chalk. Using the side of the chalk, rub it into the salt. The salt will change color. The more this is done, the greater the intensity of color.

4. Have students take turns making the "sand" until you have plates of each color.

5. This step takes time. The glue must dry between each application. Use the point of the glue to cover the sections that are going to be the same color. Sprinkle the colored salt over your painting.

6. Wait about 5 minutes (longer if the children have used a lot of glue). Gently tip and tap the excess salt onto the newspaper.

7. Repeat steps 5 and 6 for new colors until your painting is complete.

Note: For additional design ideas, refer to the bibliography on page 80.

Colored sand may be purchased at aquarium stores and used in place of the salt in this project.

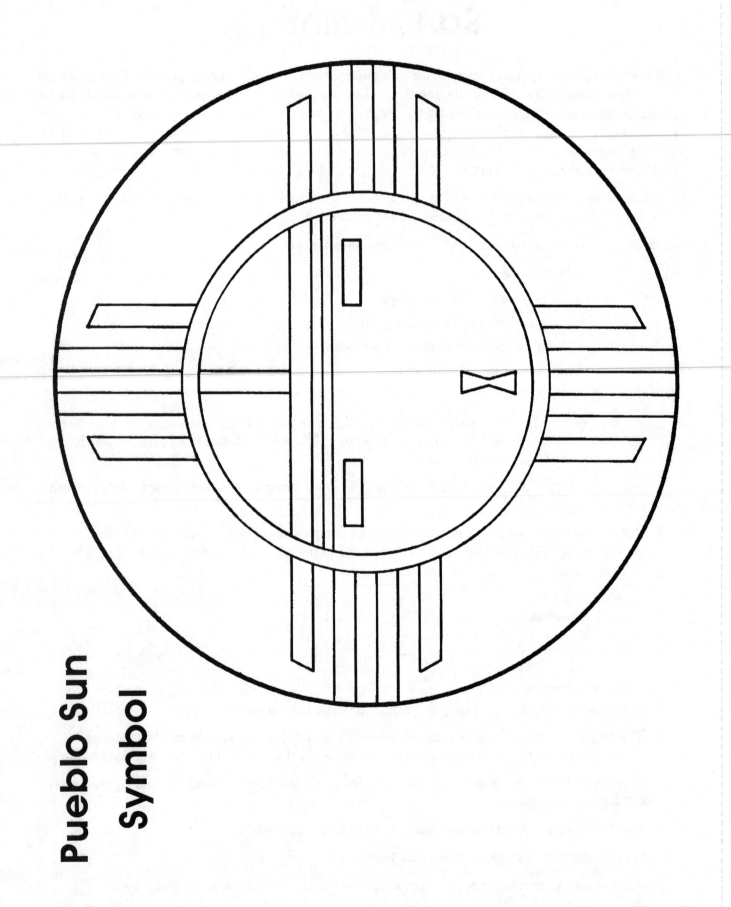

Pueblo Sun Symbol

Weaving

Weaving is a universal art practiced by all Native American tribes in one form or another. There are numerous weaving projects that are exceptionally valuable for children. Here is one that uses natural materials for the loom and some of the weaving.

Materials: branches (one per class or group)

warp string (cotton string works best since it doesn't stretch)

weft threads

bits and pieces of cloth, dried flowers, weeds, twigs, bark, seedpods, other interesting natural materials

yarn

Directions:

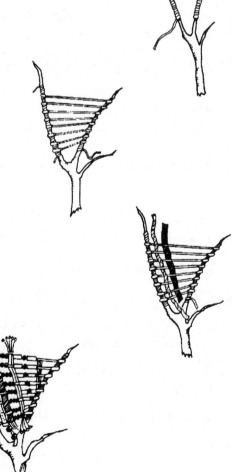

1. Use green branches from deciduous trees. They will bend more easily without splitting or breaking. Prune away twigs and side branches until you have a shape you can work with.

2. Decide where the weaving will go. Wrap that area with yarn. It will be more colorful and will keep the warp strings from slipping.

3. Using cotton string, make the loom. Knot the string around the branch, string it to the other side, wrap it around twice, go back to the original side. In this manner, go back and forth until you have created the desired size of weaving surface. Tie a knot to secure.

4. Repeat the process on the other sections of the branch.

   Hint: Steps 1-4 are best done by an adult.

5. Have students take turns weaving threads and bits and pieces onto the branch. When a student is finished with a thread or piece of yarn, have them cut it leaving at least 1-2 inches extra. This is so it can be woven back into the loom. Otherwise, it can unravel.

6. Add beads, bells, or seeds to finish the design.

Kachina Doll

The Native Americans of the Southwest have traditionally made Kachina dolls. They are symbols of a wide variety of elements in tribal life. The dolls are styled after actual Kachina dancers that wear colorful masks and costumes while they impersonate spirit beings (Kachinas).

To make the most of this project, obtain some books with pictures of actual dolls. (See Bibliography, page 80.)

Spool Kachina

Materials: wooden spools in a variety of sizes and shapes (from home or a craft store)

tempera paints and brushes

chipboard or cardboard

foam craft ball 3/4" (2cm) diameter, to use for head

scissors, glue, odds and ends

Directions:

1. Put spools together to form a person's shape.

2. When you are pleased with the shape, glue them together. Use the foam craft ball for a head.

3. When the doll is dry, add finishing touches with paint, feathers, and odds and ends.

4. If the doll is unsteady, glue to a chipboard base.

Kachina Paper Doll

Materials: 2 copies of the pattern on page 63; scissors; glue; stapler; newspaper (torn into small pieces); crayons and markers; decorations (feathers, material, old jewelry)

Directions:

1. Cut two Kachina shapes for the front and back.

2. Color the front and back of the Kachina with crayons and/or markers.

3. Staple and glue the sides together leaving an area at the top and bottom open.

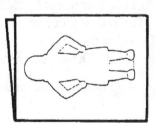

4. Stuff the doll with small bits of newspaper and staple together.

5. Glue decorations on the Kachina for added interest.

Kachina Doll Pattern

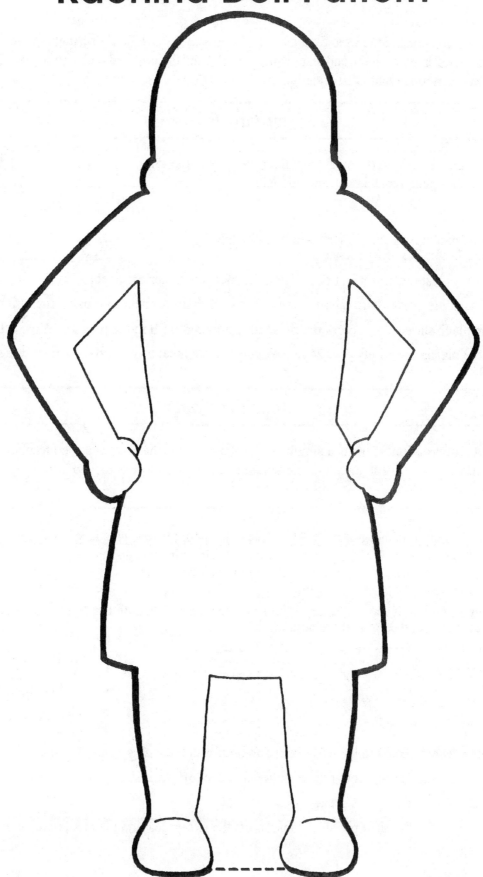

Scrimshaw

This is a very famous technique used by the Innuit (or Eskimo). Originally scrimshaw illustrated themes and stories engraved in ivory (teeth and tusks from animals) and then rubbed with lampblack. These projects are two dimensional to simulate that technique.

Scrimshaw Picture

Materials: plaster of Paris; meat container or shoe box top; dull pencil; black wax shoe polish

Directions:

1. Have students draw a simple scene (only a few lines) depicting Innuit life on a practice paper.

2. Prepare the plaster of Paris and pour it into the meat container or shoebox lid.

3. When plaster is almost hard (about 5 minutes), scratch the scene into it using the dull pencil.

4. Rub the black shoe polish across the finished engraving to fill in the picture. Wipe off the excess.

5. When the plaster is entirely dry (24 hours), remove the meat tray or box. Display the finished project.

Scrimshaw Tooth

Background Information: This is a simulation of the carvings the Eskimos used to make on whale teeth. In this project, a tooth is constructed and then a scene is carved into it.

Material:

plaster of Paris; clay (modeling or pottery); coffee can; spoon; water; plastic spray sealer; nail or tip of large paper clip; black wax shoe polish; rolling pin; orange juice can

Directions:

1. Roll out a triangle of clay and shape it into a hollow cone. Smooth the inside of the cone. Set it in the juice can with the point at the bottom.

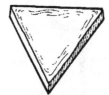

2. Mix the plaster of Paris in the coffee can and pour it into the clay cone. Let it set overnight.

3. When the plaster is dry, lift out the "tooth" and peel off the clay.

4. Using a nail, carve a simple scene into the tooth

5. Cover the tooth with shoe polish. Then rub off the excess leaving the etching design in black.

6. Spray with sealer.

     64

Pattern Poems and Songs

Since Native Americans spent a lot of their time hunting, the following song can easily be adapted for use during this unit.

> *A-hunting we will go*
> *A-hunting we will go*
> *We'll catch a fox*
> *And put him in a box*
> *A-hunting we will go*

Work together to replace lines 3 and 4 with new rhyming couplets. Have students help you list animals that Native Americans might go hunting for, such as deer, squirrel, bear, and snake. Put these words across the top of a large sheet of butcher paper. Beneath each of the words, have children assist you to create a rhyming word bank.

Rhyming Word Bank						
moose	**fish**	**hare**	**squirrel**	**deer**	**snake**	**raccoon**
loose	dish	pear	curl	tear	lake	June
goose	wish	bear	hurl	fear	bake	moon
spruce		fair	girl	hear	rake	soon
juice		stare	pearl	here	steak	loon
papoose		chair	uncurl	near	stake	tune
reduce		stair			take	noon

Here are some samples of replacements for lines three and four.

> *We'll catch a fish*
> *And put it on a dish*

> *We'll catch a hare*
> *And eat it with a pear.*

> *We'll catch a squirrel*
> *With its tail in a curl*

> *We'll catch a snake*
> *And take it home to bake.*

> *We'll catch a raccoon*
> *By the light of the moon*

> *We'll catch a deer*
> *After looking far and near*

After learning these verses, students can copy and illustrate the animal hunted using the torn construction paper technique. These verses can make a colorful bulletin board, Big Book, or a beginning reading tool.

Use the following page for students to copy verses and/or create their own verses.

A-hunting We Will Go

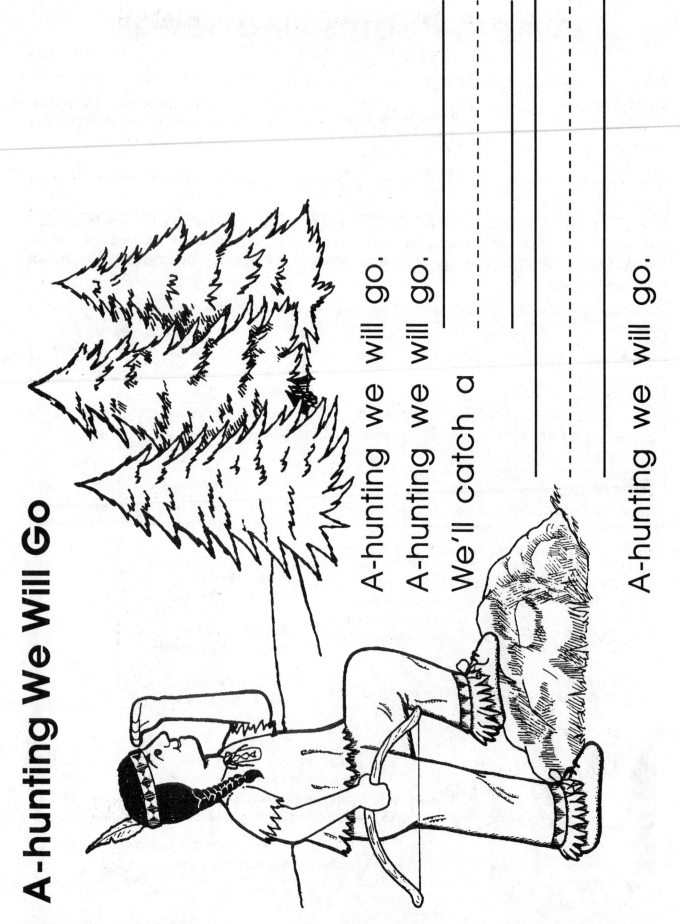

A-hunting we will go.
A-hunting we will go.
We'll catch a

A-hunting we will go.

66

Native American Musical Instruments

Music plays an important part in the life of the Native American. From the time he is born until he dies, his life is marked by dancing and ceremony. The drum provides the rhythm and is often joined by rattles and rasps to furnish the background for the chants and dances that accompany tribal ceremonies.

Drums

There are four major types of drums: the small hand drum which could be carried into battle, the larger drum usually made from a hollowed log, the water drum used by the Apache, and the basket drum used by Southwestern tribes. The drum heads are usually made from hides. The drums are decorated with painted symbols and designs having religious or protective meanings. The Native American never plays the hide drums by tapping with his hand — this is an African method. A drumstick is always used.

1. Coffee cans with plastic lids (metal bottoms removed), oatmeal boxes, salt boxes, or paper ice cream containers are instant drum material. Cover with construction paper. Add Native American symbols and designs.

2. Pottery jars, flower pots, and metal buckets also make excellent drums. Dampen and tie on a head of light 100% cotton canvas. These drums should be struck with beaters. A wooden kitchen spoon with painted Native American designs works well.

3. For a basket drum, use a woven basket. Turn it over. This can be struck by hand or with pine needles to make a whisk-like sound.

Native American Musical Instruments *(cont.)*

Rattles

Rattles were very important to the Native Americans. Medicine men shook special rattles in ceremonies and healing rituals. Rattles were used as musical instruments during dances and as background to singers. A birchbark rattle accompanied the mournful chant of a Northwest tribal funeral. The Navajo used a combination drumstick rattle made from rawhide soaked around sand and pebbles which could give a drum and rattle sound. Bright paint, feathers, colored ribbon, beads and shells were used to beautify these instruments.

Nineteenth century Native Americans prized the empty metal spice boxes used by the settler. Tin cans and other metal containers were used for rattles also.

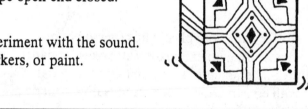

1. Make a rattle from a cardboard tube. Tape one end of the tube (paper towel, etc.) closed. Place beans inside. Shake to determine sound. Add beans until desired sound is achieved. Tape open end closed. Decorate with marking pens.

2. Use a metal, lidded box. Put in beans and experiment with the sound. Tape box lid closed. Decorate with paper, markers, or paint.

Rasps

The rasp (a notched stick) is used by many Native American tribes. By notching sticks in different ways, tribes can vary the sounds and create new sounds to accompany their dances and ceremonies.

The Sioux were able to create sound used in the Bear Dance by rubbing a short heavy rasp with another stick. This was done over a metal sheet covering a hole in the ground. Using this sounding chamber, they created a growl representing the angry spirit of a charging bear.

To make a rasp, use a piece of corrugated cardboard carton. Rub a pencil or small stick over it to create a sound.

Native American Games

All games can be played indoors or outdoors, except for Danger Signal which should be played outdoors.

Tossing and Catching Games

◆ *Bowl Catch:* Variations found in all areas of the Americas

The Native Americans played this game with a bowl and pottery disks, beaver or muskrat teeth, fruit pits, or bone depending on the area. One side of the object was plain and the other had designs which established its value.

Materials: shallow basket (8" to 10"/20 to 25cm across); 6 large lima beans

With a marker draw a Native American symbol on one side of each bean. Put the beans in the bowl. Sitting cross-legged, hold the bowl in both hands. Toss the beans into the air. Catch them in the bowl. Count those that land design side up, this is your score. Depending on the age and ability of the students, the symbols can be assigned a value and it can become a math game.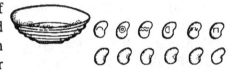

◆ *Toss and Catch:* Played by Plains, Woodlands, and Northwest Coast tribes

This game, played with sticks or reeds about 3 to 4 inches (7.5 to 10cm) long and $\frac{1}{8}$ to $\frac{1}{4}$ inch (.3 to .6cm) in diameter, was popular with boys and girls. Using craft sticks, balance two on the back of your hand at waist level. Toss the sticks straight up into the air to about head height and catch them in the palm of your hand. To increase difficulty add more sticks, turn around before catching the sticks, or catch the sticks with your palm open.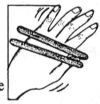

Hunting and Stalking Games

◆ *Danger Signal:* Played by Plains, Woodland, and Northwest Coast tribes

To develop hunting skills, young braves were taken into a fairly dense forest and told to spread out in various directions. They were told to listen for danger signals such as those given by alarmed birds or animals. At the sound of the alarm they were to freeze or head quickly for the cover of a tree or rock. Divide the class into thirds: braves, rocks, trees. Position yourself (as chief) at the finish line. Rocks and trees are stationary. The braves begin at the starting line. The chief turns his back and the braves move from rock to tree quickly and quietly. The chief blows a whistle, turns around, and tries to spot a brave. Braves should be frozen behind a tree or rock or they are out. The winner is the first brave to cross the finish line.

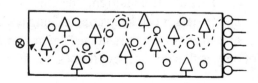

Native American Games *(cont.)*

◆ *Rattler:* Played by Plains, Woodland, Northwest Coastal,and Southwest tribes

Since rattlesnakes are found throughout the Americas, this game was developed in many forms by numerous tribes.

Have the class form a large circle, about 20 feet (6 meters) in diameter. Select two volunteers: rattlesnake and hunter. Blindfold the snake and the hunter. Place them about 10 feet (3 meters) apart within the circle. Give the rattlesnake a baby rattle or a maraca. Both students start moving. At a given interval, approximately 15 seconds, the group hisses. The rattlesnake needs to rattle at each hiss. The hunter tries to touch the snake to win the game. After this happens, select a new rattler and hunter.

Important Safety Precaution: Since the players are blindfolded, they need to move slowly and carefully, listening for each other. If the chief (you) shouts STOP!, all action must freeze.

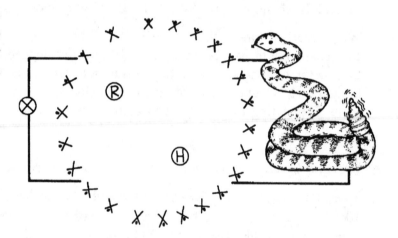

◆ *Guardian of the Fire:* Played by Plains, Woodland, and Northwest Coastal tribes

Student sits cross-legged and blindfolded in the center of the circle. In front of him, within easy reach is a dowel or a ruler. This is the fire stick! The chief selects a student to try to steal the fire stick. The Guardian listens carefully with his hands on his knees. If he touches the person in the act of taking the stick, he wins the game. If not, the Guardian tries to guess who stole the fire stick. If he doesn't, the thief becomes the next Guardian.

◆ *There!:* Played by Plains and Woodlands tribes

Counting coup was a way in which a warrior could prove his bravery. Often this was accomplished by touching an enemy.

The "enemy" sits like the Guardian above. All others form a circle. The chief signals someone from the circle to be a stalker who tries to touch the enemy on the tips of the fingers without being heard. The "enemy" listens. When he thinks he hears a stalker, he points in the direction of the sound and shouts, "There." If he is right, the chief selects a new stalker. If the "enemy" points in the wrong direction, the stalker can keep approaching and the "enemy" needs to keep listening. Be sure that the students know they cannot rush the "enemy" and count coup before the person has time to say, "There!" Not only is this not fair, but it does not demonstrate bravery!

70

Native American Slapjacks

Ingredients: 1 egg

1 cup of milk

½ cup of yellow cornmeal

½ cup of flour

½ teaspoon salt

1 tablespoon shortening
butter
sugar

Directions:

1. Crack an egg into a bowl.

2. Add one cup of milk.

3. Beat the egg and milk together.

4. Add ½ cup of yellow cornmeal.

5. Add ½ cup of flour.

6. Add ½ teaspoon of salt.

7. Turn electric skillet on to 350 degrees.

8. Put a tablespoon of shortening into the skillet.

9. Drop the batter by tablespoons into the hot skillet.

10. When the edges look done, turn and cook the other side.

11. Put your slapjacks on a paper plate.

12. Put butter and sugar on them.

13. Eat and clean up.

Be a Storyteller

Storytelling is one of the greatest traditions of Native Americans. The storyteller is not only an artist, he is a magician and a creator. Most importantly, he is a holy man.

Stories are a way of explaining things. They show the relationship between man and nature. As the stories have been written down, they have recorded history; but something is lost in only reading the words. These stories teach lessons and are best enjoyed by being told.

An exciting culminating activity is to give your class the opportunity to become storytellers. Let them retell the stories studied throughout the unit or introduce a new one.

Preparation: Read several Native American legends to your class. There are many books with these ancient legends. *Keepers of the Earth* by Michael J. Caduto and Joseph Bruchac is an excellent source of tales. *Old Indian Legends* retold by Zitkala-Ša has several stories told by Dakota storytellers. *In the Beginning* told by Virginia Hamilton has some Native American creation stories. *Ten Little Rabbits* by Virginia Grossman and Sylvia Long, while not a legend in the sense of the others, is a counting book that uses weaving, fishing, and storytelling to share Native American traditions. (This would be an excellent source for young, beginning readers.)

Allow several days for preparation and presentation. Have the students make storyteller bags, a tradition of the Iroquois storytellers. They can fill these bags with props for their legends. Give them time to memorize and practice telling their legends with the use of their props. Spread the storytelling over a few days, so each student listens and participates. See page 73 for specific directions.

Be a Storyteller *(cont.)*

Materials: legend; paper bag; crayons or markers; scissors; glue; paper; scraps of fabric, yarn, feathers, beads, etc.

Directions: Help each student choose a legend that they want to tell to the class. Give each student a paper bag to decorate with crayons or markers. These will be their storyteller bags. Have the students use materials you provide to create the props for their legends.

In preparing your students for this activity demonstrate what storytelling is all about. Tell your class a story, don't read it. Begin by choosing a Native American legend. Read it out loud to yourself several times. Make a storyteller bag and props. When you are ready to tell your story, have the children sit quietly in a circle to listen to the story. Let your listeners take an active part in the story. As you tell the story and take out the props, let the children help you. Have them echo your words. Use lots of expression in telling your story. Choose a standard beginning and ending for your stories as many Native Americans did. "Would you like to hear a story" as a beginning and "This is all," as an ending, are used by many Native Americans.

To give you some ideas here is an example using *Ten Little Rabbits* by Virginia Grossman and Sylvia Long.

Child: Would you like to hear a story?

Audience: Yes.

Child: This is a story about ten little rabbits. (pause)

"One lonely traveler riding on the plain." (Hold up one finger.)

"Two graceful dancers asking for some rain." (Take out flowers and dance around.)

"Three busy messengers sending out the news." (Take out a piece of fabric and pretend to send smoke signals.)

The child continues in this way to the end of the story and closes by saying "This is all."

Creating a Room Environment

As you proceed through this Native American unit, you will be enjoying literature selections from three of the eight basic tribal areas of North America. After studying each area, fill in a wall chart of Native American facts. By having this chart created as the children study, it becomes a comprehension and analysis tool.

You will need space, yarn, and labels. (Use a bulletin board or a large butcher paper chart.)

Native American Information Chart						
Area	Map	Tribes	Transportation	Food	Shelter	Notes

1. With yarn, make a grid as shown above. Put up the column labels as indicated.

2. Make eight copies of the tribal area map on page 76. Outline a different tribal area on each one with black marker.

3. Put area labels and matching maps in the first two columns. (See page 75.)

4. As you study each area, add the information to the wall chart in a format students understand — words, pictures, or a combination.

5. Reproduce student chart from page 77. Have students record the information from the wall chart.

6. On a daily basis, review the information on the chart. By the completion of the unit, the students will have a sound basic knowledge of Native American facts.

Native American Display Area: Send home a parent letter requesting artifacts to use in a display area.

Native American Reference Area: Check out library books and display students' books. Encourage use during social studies period and sustained silent reading.

Native American Reference Chart

Unit Management

Area	Map	Tribes	Transportation	Food	Shelter	Notes
Arctic/Subarctic	(See page 74 #2 and 3 for map directions.)	Innuit, Aleut	Dog sled, snowshoe, kayak, toboggan	Caribou, moose, bear, deer, fish	Hide or bark covered wigwams or tepees, igloos	Most tribes were hunters and fishermen
Northwest Coastal		Tlingit, Haida, Yurok, Tsimshian, Kwakiutl, Nootka, Salish, Hupa	Canoe, foot	Fish, caribou, roots, moose, berries	Longhouses made from wood	Fishermen, made totem poles
Plateau		Nez Perce, Yakima, Flathead, Spokan	Foot, dugout canoe, (later) horse	Fish, deer, roots, berries, bison	Longhouses, circular houses built partly into the ground	Foragers, noted for baskets
Great Basin		Comanche, Ute, Klamath, Paiute, Shoshoni, Washo	Foot, dog travois, (later) horse	Seeds, roots, ants, snake, berries, pine nut, locust, lizard, mice, rabbit, deer	Tepees	Land inhospitable, on constant verge of starvation
California		Modoc, Pomo, Yana, Chumash	Foot	Acorns, plant foods, shellfish, fish, small game	Rounded, grass-covered houses	Foragers, basket makers, lived in relatively mild climate
Plains & Prairie		Arapaho, Pawnee, Crow, Blackfoot, Sioux	Foot, horse, dog travois	Bison, other game	Portable tepees in summer, permanent tepees in villages in winter	Excellent horsemen, buffalo hunters, more warlike
Eastern Woodlands		Erie, Huron, Mohawk, Delaware, Kickapoo, Shawnee, Iroquois	Foot, canoe	Fish, game, wild rice, maple sugar	Longhouse	Large area – from northeastern Canada to Florida – sometimes divided into Eastern Woodland and Southeast
Southwest		Navajo, Pueblo, Hopi, Zuni, Apache	Foot	Wild plants, small animals, maize	Hogan (Navajo), Multistory "apartment houses"	Cultivators and foragers

Tribal Regions of North America

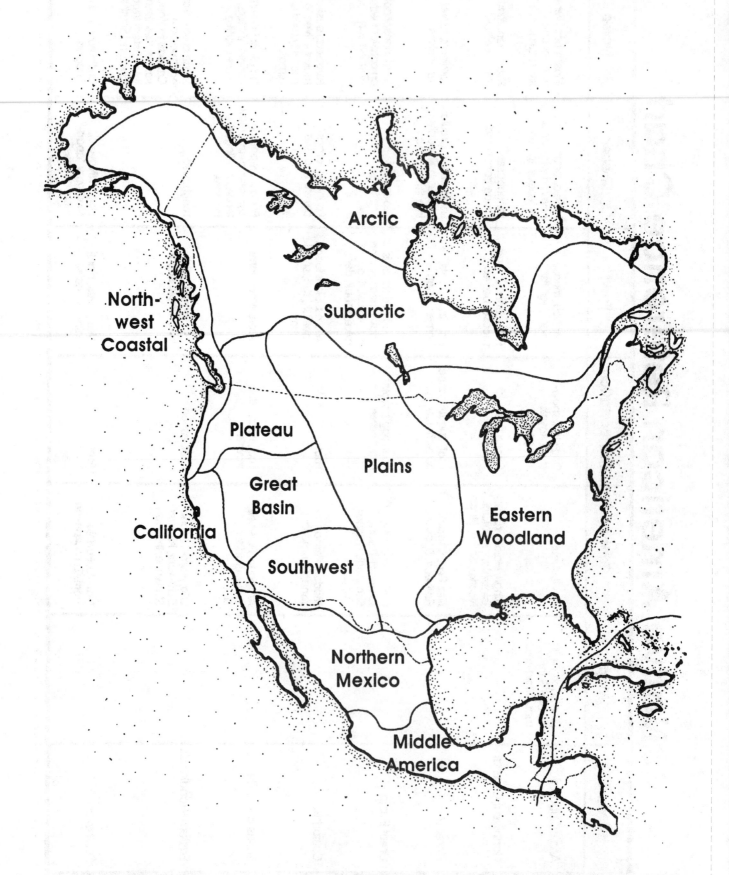

Charting Native Americans Facts

Area	Tribes	Transportation	Food	Shelter	Other Facts

Bulletin Boards

Create bulletin boards to display your students' work throughout the Native American unit. Two suggestions are given below.

Poetry of Colors Bulletin Board

Create a bulletin board to display the poetry that students write during the Native American unit. Title the bulletin board ''Poetry of Colors.'' Write the title in different colors or cut letters out of different colored construction paper. As students finish writing poems (see page 37) add them to the poetry display.

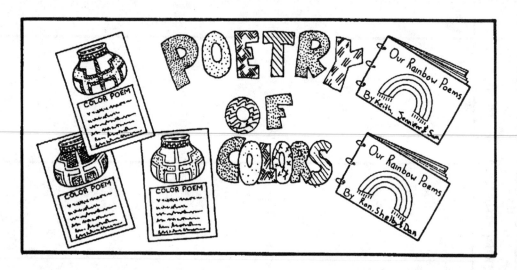

Our Native American Artists Bulletin Board

The Native American thematic unit includes many art projects. Display student work on a colorful bulletin board. Title the bulletin board ''Our Native American Artists.'' You may decorate the letters. As students complete art projects (Kachina, p. 62, Totem Pole, p. 57) hang them up. If possible place a table nearby to display art projects that cannot be mounted such as the Class Totem Pole (p. 58) or Scrimshaw (p. 64).

Awards

Tribal Tribute

To: _____

For: _____

_____

_____

_____

_____

_____ _____

Teacher's Signature   Date

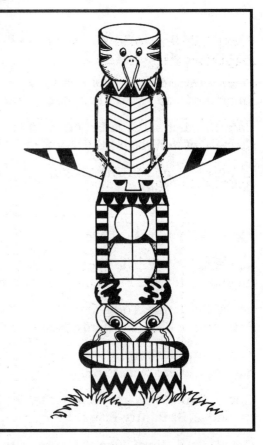

OFFICIAL
Fantastic Feather
AWARD

For Fantastic Work!

_____

_____

_____

_____ _____

Teacher's Signature   Date

Bibliography

Baylor, Byrd. *When Clay Sings*. (Charles Scribner's Sons, 1972)

Beierhorst, John. *Doctor Coyote: A Native American Aesop's Fables*. (Macmillan, 1987)

Caduto, Michael J. & Bruchac, Joseph. *Keepers of the Earth*. (Fulcrum, Inc., 1989)

Cleaver, Elizabeth. *The Enchanted Caribou*. (Atheneum, 1985)

DeArmond, Dale. *Berry Woman's Children*. (Greenwillow Press, 1985)

de Paola, Tomie. *The Legend of the Bluebonnet*. (G.P. Putnam's Sons, 1983)

de Paola, Tomie. *The Legend of the Indian Paintbrush*. (G.P. Putnam's Sons, 1988)

Esbensen, Barbara Juster. *Ladder to the Sky*. (Little, Brown, 1989)

Gobel, Paul. *The Great Race of the Birds and Animals*. (Bradbury Press, 1985)

Gobel, Paul. *Her Seven Brothers*. (Bradbury Press, 1988)

Gobel, Paul. *Iktomi and the Berries*. (Orchard Books, 1989)

Grossman, Virginia & Long, Sylvia. *Ten Little Rabbits*. (Chronicle Books, 1991)

Hoyt-Goldsmith, Diane. *Totem Pole* (Holiday, 1990)

Lacapa, Michael. *The Flute Player*. (Northland Publishing, 1990)

Longfellow, Henry Wadsworth. *Hiawatha*. (Dial Books, 1983)

McDermott, Gerald. *Arrow to the Sun*. (Viking Press, 1974)

Morgan, William. *Navajo Coyote Tales* (Ancient City Press, 1988)

Roth, Susan L. *Kanahena, A Cherokee Story*. (St. Martin Press, 1988)

Scott, Ann Herbert. *On Mother's Lap*. (McGraw-Hill, 1972)

Steptoe, John. *The Story of Jumping Mouse*. (Lothrop, Lee & Shepard, 1984)

Troughton, Joanna. *Who Will be the Sun?*. (Peter Bedrick Books, distributed in the USA by Harper and Row, 1985)

Van Laan, Nancy. *Rainbow Crow*. (Knopf, 1989)

Hamilton, Virginia. *In the Beginning: Creation Stories from Around the World*. (Harcourt Brace Jovanovich, 1988)

Zitkala-Ša. *Old Indian Legends*. (University of Nebraska Press, 1985)

Reference Books

Asch, Connie. *Indian Dancers Coloring Book*. (1982)

Asch, Connie. *Katchina Coloring Book*. (1982)

> Both books can be ordered through: Treasure Chest Publications, Inc. 1842 W Grant Road, Suite 107, P.O. 5250, Tucson, AZ 85703.

Bahti, Mark. *Navaho Sandpainting Art*. (Walsworth Publishing Company, 1978)

Fordham, Derek. *Eskimos*. (Macdonald Educational, 1979)

Macfarlan, Allan, and Paulette. *Handbook of American Indian Games*. (Dover Publications, Inc., 1958)

Smith, J.H. Greg. *Eskimos-The Inuit of the Arctic*. (Rourke Publications, Inc., 1987)